HOW GOD CHANGED MY LIFE

How God Changed My Life
Published by KJM Publishing

www.facebook.com/kishajordanKJM
www.kishajordanenterprises.org

ISBN: 9798846749900

TABLE OF CONTENTS

DEDICATION

I dedicate this book to my Father
I dedicate this book to Jesus Christ
I dedicate this book to the Holy Ghost

BECAUSE GOD HAS kept me through all my bad mistakes, through the sweat, the blood, and the tears for 46 years of my foolishness. God has given me more grace and mercy than I can imagine. Today, this is why I will serve him, and I'll serve him for the rest of my life. What is important to me is getting the work done for Christ, dying empty when my time comes, and knowing that God is pleased with me and with the job he has given me to do for his Glory.

INTRODUCTION

I WROTE THIS book because God commanded me to. I wrote this book for God's glory because he spoke to his prophetess and told me to write it to save the lives of his people. God wanted me to write this book to save, change, correct, and deliver his people and to encourage them for his glory. That is why it is so important to follow the instructions of God.

God said he chose me before the foundation of the world. He said he is bringing me to the forefront of the world. The Chosen One has sent this book to bring this to the forefront of the world. He is using this book for His glory. What Satan meant for evil; God is turning it out for His glory. Not for my benefit but for His glory.

When God spoke to me regarding this book, I said, "Yes, God, I will do it and will go because you have sent me into the world to preach the gospel. For you can, do, and will move through me God of the living God." Jesus is the son of the living God, and the Holy Spirit is the helper and trainer. He is the action of God.

CHAPTER 1
Country Girl Seduced by a Different World

I WAS BORN in Arkansas on July 16, 1961. I'm a sibling of 10 children. I am the fifth child. I was raised by my grandmother. She was a beautiful, righteous, trustworthy, and honest woman. She was faithful to the Lord and she loved her daughter and grandchildren.

Her life was surrounded by God, her man, and her grandkids. She told us about God, Jesus, the Holy Spirit, and going to church. We had to go to church every Sunday, and on the weekday, when we had choir practice. We went to school. We were not allowed to spend the night away from home unless it was someone my grandmother knew and trusted.

My grandma paid her bills on time. Water, stove bill, washer, and dryer, and insurance bill. To do so, she worked every day of the week, but Saturday, the Sabbath day. That was always a day of rest. She took us shopping for dress shoes and nylon.

A friend of my mother' had a farm. My brother, sister, and I would go to the farm on the weekend. She and I would sleep in the same bed and pray for each other. While we were there, we would help her on the farm. She and I would work my sister and brother until they sweat, while she and I would sit down under the shade and drink iced tea, and lemonade, and eat cake.

They did tell Mom Dear about what was going on. Then, one day, my grandmother straightened us out really quickly.

So, my life consisted of playing on the railroad tracks, spending time in the alley, and sitting down to talk to God.   It also consisted of running with a childhood friend, Diana. She was bad and so was I.

She would take her mom's food stamps and we would go to the grocery store to shop. As soon as my grandmother found out about it, she would come to the store. She would whip anyone's children when they were doing wrong. She would take them home to their parents. My grandmother was trustworthy. I was always getting a whooping for being with her and doing something wrong. She would run away from home.

My uncle would come down to our house every morning at 7:00 a.m. and whip me, then he would go to work. I would wet the bed. So, my grandmother took me to the doctor to see if I had a bladder infection to see why I could not stop wetting the bed. When the doctor found nothing was wrong, I got another whipping, and it was much harder.

There was a woman that would come to our house every now and then in a big fancy car. She would be with a tall man. She would have toys, gifts, clothes, and train sets for my brothers. I thought she was a fairy godmother because every time I would lose a tooth she would come. It looked that way and this went on for a very long time.

She would stay there with us, but I would not hear anything said. She would talk to my grandmom privately, so everything was a secret.

She raised my sister. My sister wasn't always with us, but we spent a lot of time together. My sister would read the Bible to us. I always knew something was different about her.

My older sister was always a mother figure for me. She always took care of me and spent time with me. However, my sister and brother never wanted me to go with them because I would tell everything I saw, such as, if they were kissing someone or if they were doing something they should not be doing, like going to the movies to meet a boyfriend.

I did not have a boyfriend or never thought of it anyway. I spent a lot of time going to the store for my uncles and family members. My aunt sang and my uncle was the base boy. My aunt worked in our church. She was an usher on the board. My pastor and his wife were very good people.

The Holy Spirit would always move in our church. People were always crying, shouting, singing, and coming to the altar. So, it was good. I love going to church. My sister also sang in the choir. I was moved by some of the words my pastor would preach, and we had to go to Bible study and learn.

I went to a Catholic school. At school, we would get paddled if we did something wrong or they would put us in a room, they called the "Eat Up Man Room". This is where bad kids went. I never wanted to go into that room. So, I was good.

My real dad was on the police force. When I did something, he would come and put me in the police car, take me to jail and lock me up for a while. Then he would take me home. I didn't care too much for him. He never did anything for me or my brother. He also had another son, but I never understood how all this took place.

Miss Foster was a close friend of my grandmother, and she had two grandsons, Jacoby and Gabriel. I liked Jacoby, but we never did anything wrong because we knew better. Our grandparents would have killed us. We did not want to take that risk because our lives depended on it. So, we remained just friends until one day my whole life changed.

It was the worst day of my life. This lady and her husband came down and this time they came to take us away. I did not understand what was going on. My grandmother explained who she was. Her daughter and we were her grandkids. She had taken care of us until she was ready for us to be with her and her husband.

I did not think that it was a good idea. My life was there in the country. That's where I wanted to spend the rest of my life. I loved the country. I did not know much of anything. I was only about 12 years old. I was still a virgin at that time, and she took us away. When I got the chance, I ran back to my grandmother's house from the gas station. But they came to get me.

Everyone there was very nice, working people. You could trust them. If it was something going on, I did not know anything. Everything was kept from me from day one. I was always treated differently than my sisters and brothers. It was like I was hated from day one. Nothing was ever said about me. Even when I got good grades, everything was always about my sister and brother.

On one occasion, I got my arm caught and broken in the washing machine because they did not want to wash my clothes. I changed clothes a lot because I didn't like being dirty. So, my grandmom came and took me to the hospital and whipped everyone. I knew she loved me.

My grandmom would tell everyone how she feels, and she did not like white people. We were taught that way but that is not the way it ends. Initially, I did not understand why she was like that. But it was because of slavery. Her mom and her family were slaves, so now I can understand. But she was a woman of God, so she would pray and be able to forgive, that's what I want to say, but I kept my mouth shut, or else I would get a whipping.

I was not allowed to say anything unless someone was talking to me. We had to address other people with "yes" or "no sir", or "yes" or "no ma'am". We never talked back to anyone. If they asked us to go to the store or do anything for them, we better do it without a word. It was yes ma'am, or sure. My lifestyle in the country was the only lifestyle I knew until we moved to Chicago.

In the country in Arkansas, everyone knew my family, my school, my church, all my friends, and all the older people whom I would go and take care of. Now, my sister, my brother, and I were leaving. We left school, my church, friends, and all the older people. Now I'm leaving. Me, my sister, and my brother. I was so sad. I felt like I had nothing to live for.

My grandma would drink beer every now and then. We would sit down on a Saturday afternoon and watch wrestling. It was family time, and we were happy. My grandmother did not abuse me. She never went to school, so she could not read or write. She had to work. Not for herself. She worked to make sure we had a roof over our heads, food, clothes, shoes, and life insurance, just in case one of us died, we would be better. It was a very quiet and comfortable life.

I was a happy child. I was very obedient when I was asked to do something because we were raised that way. It was the best any child could ask or hope for. I was happy to be in the family that God had given me.

I thought, even as a child, that I was so ugly and skinny with big eyes and really bad hair. I felt like I was cheap from the start, but I always knew, "God made us, and He did not make mistakes" as my mother dear would say. She was and still is the best woman, sister, mom, and grandma, anyone could ever ask for. I love her to the day I die. God bless her for my life in Helena, Arkansas on 221 Street Francis Street. God bless them.

Street life in Chicago

I lived in Chicago, Illinois, with my mom and her husband. We lived at 5251 South Carpenter Street on the south side of Chicago. It was me, my three brothers, and my three sisters and from day one I didn't feel right in the house or living in a big city. I had never been to a big city, and I did not understand anything about it. It was very confusing. I didn't understand it or know what was going on.

I was now 13 years old. I shared a room with my sister or sometimes I slept in the bed with my brother. I play wrestled with them. My mom had another baby. It was a little boy and the next year she had another baby, and it too was a boy. The following year or so she had a little girl. Now there were 10 of us.

I got up one morning and everyone was at the kitchen table, drinking coffee and eating. I noticed something strange on the table. It was white. I had never seen anything like that before, so I wanted to know what it was. But I kept quiet. I called my grandmother and told her what I had seen. She needed to call my mom to ask her about what was going on, and she whipped me. I knew it was wrong for her to beat me for what was true.

So, I knew my life was going nowhere. This was a different world from where I came from. I did not know how to deal with this or talk to these people. They were strangers to me, and I did not trust them. My sister was acting differently, everyone around me was different from me. Everything was a secret or code language.

Learning the Game

That's when my stepdad sat me down and begin to teach me about what was going on. He taught me about the game. He taught me about the drug world. He taught me about mixing and weighing drugs, how to cut off the key, how to sift them, how to pack them up, and how to move and to know the way to take them.

He taught me how to keep people from knowing what's going on. I learned how to carry a gun. How to unload, load, move fast, to be quick, and to shake and mix it. I learned how to answer the door, to push drugs. Your money first and who you serve. I learned to pay attention to what is going on around me.

At that time, I was attending Sherman Elementary School. I was dressing in $300 suits, $400 shoes, and $200 to $300 hair laid to the side with finger weave. Very sharp. A shaker.

I could make a man do anything I wanted them to do because of my body and I knew how to use it very well. I knew it was good and different. I had been different from day one and wore a lot of jewelry. I was always chauffeured and had a sugar daddy. At that time, I was 14 to 15 years old.

CHAPTER 2
The Spirit of Prostitution

I GOT INVOLVED with prostitutes, drug dealers, women lovers, thieves, liars, and robbers. I was running with people that would put hits on each other. Now I had learned the game to 95%. So, I knew how to shake and spoke grass, and pop green acid. I lived a life as a call girl.

I started working the streets on Sheridan Road up north and was dedicated to my women. I had a boyfriend for just a little while for him to take my virginity and that was all. He really didn't care about me. He just wanted to see what he can get. I got my virginity taken on top of a pool table.

I was so into this lifestyle until I was so comfortable that I could not see daylight if it slapped me in the face. I had the attitude that I was the baddest girl in town. I had lots of tricks coming and going. I had 20 to 30 tricks, having sex using condoms. I knew how to use my body and looks to get the job done.

From downtown Lakeshore Lake Point Tower and Palmer's House Millionaire Club, in and out of every hotel from high end to low end. Now I am dining in fancy restaurants with $200 to $300 a plate, with the millionaire mob pushing kilos and gun money.

Falling in Love with a
Gang Leader

I was in love with Xavier. He was a major gang leader. He was in the mob and was one of the biggest dope dealers in Chicago. He and four brothers. He was one of the coldest pimps I had ever known. He had Mercedes-Benzes, Rolls-Royces, Lamborghinis, Jaguars, Lincoln Town cars, and big limousines on the south side of Chicago.

Chapter 2
The Spirit of Prostitution

It was so sewed up and put together that they paid the police off. Family hustlers, they were the coldest, and they were married. Big mansions and they had girls that knew it and they were down with them because they were real with everything and everybody.

They were tall and well-dressed. They wore gator shoes, snake shoes, crocodile shoes, and tailored suits. Long black hair, finger waves, big diamond rings, and silk socks. They owned a record store and a candy store. Their mother was well taken care of.

They shut the southside down. They had dope houses everywhere. I worked at one when I spent time with him. I knew he had 15 other women, and I was not worried about what he was doing because I already knew when hits were going to be made. Where people were going and what was going to happen. When the dope was coming and how it was being distributed. I loved him very much.

Up north of us, the Italian mob was killed. Everyone in the family. They were shipping drugs in and out of the city. Nolan was holding down the west side, one of the biggest dope dealers in Chicago was doing all drop-offs, put-off, and putting hits on people that were not following orders.

If you snitched, you died that night or that week. You execute the hit with silence or burn up, or straight to the heart. Kids even got it. If they could find your family, they would die.

Winston was holding down the west side. He was making his move. Having hits put on or take off execution-style. Sex, money, and drugs controlled everything. Police, judge, and lawyers were paid to do their job.

Prosecutors were paid off. The jail was paid off. Hitmen were paid off and I did not know when the hit was taking place or where it was done. Very professional, without a trace, without anyone around or knowing anything.

You had to die by the mob game. Don't leave anyone alive or if you did, they would have someone kill you until the job was done. You were paid well. You had to be trusting.

Most of all, you had to be loyal to your family in the mob. That is the way of the mob world. After a hit was made, they always had a witness when someone was killed, put in the trunk of a car, or found in a river or lake or wooded areas sitting in the car with a bullet to the head or heart or execution-style.

There was the Black mob, Italian mob, Mexican mob, Latin mob, Iran mob, and a White mob. Everyone had their people in place to get the job done.

Women were used a lot because the oldest profession was to go into a bar, top shops, or wherever they were and have conversations with whoever to make a date or arrange to meet again. Set it up at the hotel, then get high or in the jacuzzi. Make sure they got the room in their name, that they are already there, and make sure you can get to the door, in and out, very fast, and don't leave any fingerprints.

The police, judges, lawyers, prosecutors, you just pay them off. From the bail, jail, prison, detectives, the paddy wagon, ambulance, to the hospital, and medical, all were paid off. Anything that moved we had control of it. Chicago was truly sold out for money, sex, and drugs, and everyone was paid off.

When things did not go as planned, the judge, police, lawyer, prosecutor, everyone was killed and someone else was hired, and it kept on going and going.

When I was going to be elected into the family, they wanted me to be a hitwoman. I had a silent gun with a scope on it. I carried it in a black case. I could dress like a lawyer and be very business savvy. I could dress like a prostitute, or like a sister or daughter. I had a lot of faces. I was fast and no one could catch me. If you looked and saw me one moment, then looked again, I would be gone.

The gangster that I fell in love with had a lot of wisdom. He was in the family, and he would own things. For me and my family, we held the south down with him. He was my daddy, my father, and we were very close.

On the east side, 60 Normal, the GD was holding it down. Damian was the leader. That's where I met my wife whom I love so much, and about three and four other women, along with a pimp daddy and mob. Selling drugs and sex controlled every man I came in contact with.

I try to take over their mind because if I get their mind, I have everything they own. I did not care who

Chapter 2
The Spirit of Prostitution

they were, where they came from, what they had, or what they stood for. I had to have what I wanted, when I wanted it, where I wanted it, how I wanted it and from who I wanted it. I was well qualified to get what I wanted and to keep it for as long as I wanted it. I loved that lifestyle, and I would have died for it.

CHAPTER 3
Every Relationship was Different

AS A LITTLE girl at the age of 14, I was willing to get my virginity taken by someone whose mother and my sister's father are sister and brother. So, I guess we were family. No one even said it was wrong. I can see this now and I'm feeling very hurt as I am writing this book.

He had one brother and one sister, and they lived on the same block as me. We went to school together and everything was good between our families. I would go to his house, and he came to my house.

We spent time together playing pool or going out. We would have family gatherings and he was invited. Birthday parties, dinner parties, or passing each other on the way to the store. I saw him all the time

We had to fight with white people to go to school until one day my boyfriend brought a gun. He was tired of fighting, he just wanted it to stop so we could just go to school. One day, on Wolcott Street during the fighting with white people, he tried to scare the guy. He tried to shoot the guy but ended up shooting his best friend.

Once I graduated from Sherman School, I went to Tilden High School on South Union Street in Chicago. One day when I was walking to my class, this guy named Lorenzo. I was cool with him, and we started going out after school to games, or out to eat.

My sister and others tried to tell me that he was not a good person. But I thought they just didn't want me to have someone, so I kept going out with him. We became very close, and I started having feelings for him.

I went to his house and met his family. I met his mom, daughter, sister, and brother. She was a single mom. We would drink, have fun, and play cards until all the playing was over. Come to find out, my mom found a picture under my pillow, and she was so upset with me. She put me on punishment.

I went out again and afterward when I tried to get into the house, my mom did not let me in. They were waiting for me, to see if I would get in, but my mom did not let me in. So, I went back over to their house, and we continue to party. I showered and put on a red negligee.

I laid down and he started to make love to me from my ear, down to my breast and licking me down my back, all around down to my thighs, down to my leg, up and straight down to my you know what, and so much more. In and out, up, and down, until I had an orgasm like I never had one before. We continued until I passed out.

The next morning, I woke up and to my surprise, I had spent the last night with a woman. My breath stopped, my heart stopped, and tears came from my eyes. My trust was stolen. Everything I believed in was destroyed and taken from me.

I start hitting her, asking her, "Why she did not tell me she was a woman?" She knew that I like men, not women. I was not raised that way. A woman sleeping with another woman was a disgrace to my family and me. "God blessed me and help me through this mess I got myself into" that was all I could think of.

I wanted to tell my sister, someone, anyone that I could trust, and for them to understand what happened. Only God knew the truth and even after I found out, I had fallen so in love with her. I could kill her, bring her back to life, and love her all over again.

I fell in love with her daughter, Quench. I took care of her, and bought her everything, I did not have any kids at that time, so she was all our baby. Her mom was a sweet single working mom, so we did what we could do for her. She had her own room so that was where I lived with her.

Leaving that Place

I left her home at the age of 15, and then all hell broke out. The truth came out. She had so many women that it was making my head swing. They did not like me, one even hated me, and they all wanted to fight me.

Lisa was going with me, and every woman there was, but I stayed because I had nowhere else to go. She and I became close, but she would go over to the home of another woman.

My family lived one block from her mom's house and Thomas' mom lived right around the corner with her. So, we all were from the hood and one of the ladies wanted to fight me many times, but I did not want to fight her. I could not understand why she wanted to fight me since she was pregnant with another man's baby.

One day, Jayden and I got into a fight and Tony jumped me. I was cool. I did not lose or win. I felt like it was not right but Lisa was the only person who could stop it, but she wants all of us.

One of the ladies wanted to straight kill her but Lisa was not having that. She did not let anyone hit someone if she was around. So, she stopped the woman who was starting the trouble from coming over there, but she would still show up without anyone knowing. My girlfriend and her would get into a fight.

We were a straight mess. Mad hurt like we did not have any family. My mom disowned me for 6 years and as a result, I felt very hurt and lost. So, I put up with the mess for 4 years of my life.

Then my girlfriend started jumping on me and fighting me. She gave me a black eye and my face was swollen. She would jump on me anytime she was angry or drunk. She would drink Wild Irish Rose and do cocaine. I would go out and sell my body, my dope and give her thousands of dollars to take care of her daughter.

She was my pimp. She would be with any woman she wanted. I accepted anything she did, and it was okay with me. But it was killing me on the inside. I was being destroyed. My heart was being crushed into millions of pieces.

As time went on, her brother wanted to have sex with me. He was drunk and she would come in and fight her brother about me. It was so crazy. I did not deserve to be treated like this. But I had no clue what to do or where to go. I was so in love with her.

Eventually, things got out of control and went from bad to worse. I realized things were not going to get better. When we went to the pub, her women would show up. We would catch a cab and go home. We went up north to the warehouse for 2 to 3 days of partying all night and day. We had such a good time. She would tell me how much she loved me and about how I have taken care of her business and daughter.

I spent a lot of time with her daughter. Bathing her, playing with her, and putting her to bed. By the time my baby came home we knew it was our time to be together, other than when she went to see her other women. She stopped them from coming over. I was very glad about that. Instead, she would go out to meet them. Mom always said she was not going to have this going at her house.

If I was going to be staying there, all the mess had to stop. Things did get better at home, but they got worse in the streets as all of us hung around in the same hood. There were always fights as she would always have women with her. So, the woman whom my girlfriend stopped from coming over to the house and I started talking to each other and she found out that we were in love with the same woman.

She had a baby. A boy and my girlfriend fell in love with him. She still loved on her, me, and everyone else. I was getting so sick and tired of her ways until I finally got so fed up with everything. I'm spending thousands and thousands of dollars, she's taking my money, spending it on her women. I was really getting upset, sick, not eating, not sleeping, losing weight, and just getting very sick, and feeling like I wanted to kill myself.

I moved in with my grandma and went to work at the chemical plant making good money. I stayed for a month or two. I would call my girlfriend from there and she wanted me to come back to her. But I was not putting up with it anymore.

So, at this time we started to put two and two together and realized my girlfriend was playing everybody. We decided to leave her.

I ran my grandma's phone bills up to $100 and she almost had a heart attack when she saw the bill. She was very angry with me. She did not understand that lifestyle. Anyways, she said it was best for me to go back home and that's what I did. I got a flight back home and went over to her house. She was in surgery, so I went to see her. Gave her some money and I left her and never looked back. The end of her.

CHAPTER 4
Going from Bad to Worse

I WAS NEW, very trustworthy, honest, open, understanding, and knowledgeable of what was going on and how things were supposed to happen. Whatever the boss said, that was it. My family and I were doing our thing. Selling drugs, holding the block down, paying police off, and getting things done.

We were stopping gangs from doing things. Doing a robbery and getting away, just was not going to happen. We didn't take anything from anyone.

No one there was a real gangster because we were the real gangsters. We didn't step back from anyone. We fight or we come to kill. It was taken care of with just a phone call. The hit was made and that was it. No return. It was cold but it was fair. That was the way the game goes.

I was very attractive and had breasts to die for. Implants had nothing on them. I could stop a car in traffic. I love women at this point and was living in my own world. It belonged to me and my folk. I married my woman. She taught me the game of "Trick-a-trick".

I got knowledge that my baby was in jail. I was so hurt. I could not imagine how he felt. Me, his mom and father, and his family, all know it was an accident. He was never the same, and we grew apart. He would always try to talk to me, and I still cared for him. He was the first man or person that touched me in a sexy way. So, yes. I fell in love with him and his family. But his mom never liked me.

My boyfriend, with whom I lost my virginity, was the pick of the kids. Even when we broke up, we were still good. From time to time, we would sit and have sex when he wanted it. He had it, I wanted it, and I got it. We had that understanding until he had a girlfriend. Her name was Martha.

His girlfriend had a little girl. A very beautiful baby.
I was very hurt about it, but I had to move on. I
understood he had to do what he needed to do.
Everyone got along and respected each other. It was
what it was until I moved to Minneapolis, Minnesota.

Then I started rolling with some who was all the
talk. I rolled with her, right or wrong. She took care of
me, but I was not right. I would do whatever I wanted
to do, and it was okay. I was messed up, very messed
up in my thinking but she was my baby. I loved her so
much.

I hurt her a lot when we lived in Chicago together.
In our home, I cooked, cleaned, washed her clothes,
and gave her money. I took care of her, just like she
took care of me. It was nothing that I would not do for
her.

One day we were drinking, playing cards, and
having fun, her family and I, and her brother. Her
brother was in the military, and he had come home.
We were just having fun. Just getting high, and
drinking.

I went to bed with him, and it was good. Remind
you, I was a lesbian that only tricked with guys for the

money. By that time, I was good at oral sex, so when it came to sexual intercourse it was over, so I didn't have to use my you know what, very much.

Between him, and her, I got pregnant and had his baby. Sadly, she died when she was 5 days old. We tried and tried to get in touch with him, but we could not reach him. When he came home, he was looking for his baby, but she had died.

Now I'm back in Chicago. I was so angry at myself and her, so it bought confusion to the family and that was not good. As time went on, I was so torn between these two. She was the baddest woman I had, and he was the best man I have ever had. I wanted both of them and I had both whenever I wanted. This went on for a long time.

Her and I then moved to Michigan. I would go anywhere with her and do anything for her because she was my baby. A very sweet person. She had a good heart and was kind. Her mother was my heart, her sister was my sister, and her brother was my brother. She put me on top of her uncle because he had money and drove a Mercedes-Benz.

Chapter 4
Going from Bad to Worse

In Michigan, he was good to me, and he gave me money. My wife and I kept this going as long as we could. Meanwhile, her brother and I had feelings for each other, and we could not keep our hands off each other.

When he came back home this time, we had sex. We would not stop. Over and over again, and I got pregnant again and had a miscarriage. It was a baby boy.

At that time, I was done with the whole thing. I kept hurting my wife. I would not put her through this anymore. She was hurt so bad. I would look at her and feel so ashamed of myself.

She wanted a baby, and I knew she wanted a baby. At this point, I had disgraced her, and I was ready to do whatever she wanted me to do. We would go to her house to clean and take care of her. She got paid for it.

Then, I met another guy named Brandon. Every day he would come and write down lottery names, and he would drink and play cards with us. He was digging me. He was nice-looking. He wanted to be with me.

He heard the talk about me losing the baby and said, "I'm not rich but I can take care of a baby, can get social security for the rest of her life, and I would understand that you and her are together. That is okay. You all think about it and let me know."

She and I talked about it, and we thought it would be a good idea since we have a good understanding, it should be okay. So, we set up a date and time for us to go over to his house. I had sex with him and got pregnant the first time and it was on. I was pregnant for the full nine months.

He took care of me and fed me. He took me to the doctor and made sure that I was okay. But my feelings got involved and I fell in love with him because I was pregnant by him. He and I started to see each other a lot and confusion came between him, her, me, and the family.

I had to do something to make her feel that she was in control. But she was not a saint and in most of the things I have done, she has played a part in it. She was the person behind the scenes. She was okay with me selling my body to get money, so I felt like I could do whatever I wanted because I was bringing the most money in.

Chapter 4
Going from Bad to Worse

I was right by her in the areas of our life, and I am sure she was talking to her ex, or the other women she would be involved with, and I was right. She was very quiet, but you must listen and watch everything she said or did. She had lots of street knowledge. But overall, I can say I was okay with her and that I love her enough to leave her and not keep hurting her.

So, I left her in Michigan and after that, she was talking to someone else. I blew it off. It hurt but not as much. As the years went by, I felt good that she was with someone and would not be alone.

I met another woman. Her name was Miss B. She was sexy to me. I like the way she carried herself. She had a job, her own place, a car, and lots of women friends. We got together and I moved in.

Her birthday was on July 12th, and mine is on the 16th, so we were the same zodiac sign. I met her mom. Her mom got me a job where she worked. She had a sister and two brothers. I loved her family very much.

We had a quiet life. She was very romantic. Giving me flowers, cards, gifts, and quiet dinners with champagne. She was very elegant and classy. I liked every quality about her.

When we made love to each other it was in a way I had never done before. I fell deeply in love with her, like I have never felt about another woman or man. She had my heart in the palm of her hands and life was good. Until one day it was not.

Cocaine took Control of My Life

I did something that I had never done before. I sold cocaine all my life but never smoked anything. Using cocaine was the biggest and worse choice that I ever made.

So, my new girlfriend said to me, "No, you don't want to do that, but I cannot stop you. I don't want you to do it." But I did. It was the first time I'd ever smoked cocaine and I fell in love with it.

After that, she did not allow me to get with her. I did not understand. So, I started to get high with other people that she did not agree with. Her and I started arguing and fighting and not seeing eye to eye. I wanted to spend the rest of my life with her. I had my daughter living with us as well, but I lost total control of my life.

Giving Up My Baby

I called my mom who lived in Minneapolis to come and get my baby. I love my baby more than life itself and I wanted her to be safe and well taken care of. She was 3 years of age at the time. My mom picked her up and took care of her. I signed her social security over to my mom.

I was so hurt by this mess that I had gotten myself into. Not my life with my girlfriend, but with the drugs. I should have listened to her, she was right.

Now, I'm writing this book about my life, and I can see what she said. I felt from day one, I wish that she had helped me to get treatment, and then afterward decide if she still wanted to be with me. I believe in my heart and soul that it would have made a difference.

We could have been friends if nothing else. Maybe we could have gotten past this. But she wanted out and I was very torn. I did not know how to deal with it. I was in love with her, and I had never loved anyone as I loved her. I even got her name tattooed on me.

It took me about 5 years to be able to not think about her, but I knew God was the one that would help me. All I could do was pray. All I knew at that time was Psalms 27. So, I held onto prayer and Psalms 27 as if my life depended on it.

I went through it and finally, she asked me to leave. She did not care where I went or whom I went with. I had to leave. I felt so betrayed. All we shared and I never in my heart knew she felt that way because of the way she handled it. What I was feeling was so real. She wanted to move on. I did not mean that much to her or anyone at that time.

But God loved me more than I ever knew. He was all I had when my own family turned their back against me, talked about me, and called me names whenever I go back there.

When she asked me to leave, I fought her, because I loved her so much. I did not know how to deal with it no other way. I broke her car windows out. It was a mess. I would ring the doorbell. If she did not answer and I knew she was at home, I knew that if I mess with her car, she will come out. I just wanted to see her and hold her and tell her all the things that I'm saying now. This was the way I felt at that time.

Time went on and I moved out of state. I could not stand to see her anymore. God would change my mind. Little did I know, He was working on me. I did not know, but when I moved, I had gotten so bad about her that I could not believe that was what I was hearing. Because of whom it came from, I felt it was true and it turned out to be true.

Over the years, God got me through it, and I was on my way to recovery. I prayed that when I get clean, He gives me the strength to see her and to say nice things to her. Not to hate her.

God, how can people do bad things to others? Help me God to understand what I did to deserve this.

I wanted to die at that point in life. Life couldn't get any worse than this. But little did I know it did get worse. Through the years, I would call her, to hear if it was true, and she said, "Yes". I said you could have done anything in this world but not this. I told her, "She would hurt me but not only through this person."

As time went on, God healed my heart and gave me strength. Day by day, step by step, moment by moment. It was the worst time in my life. I was dealing with my addiction, but I had to move on.

I was still a child. It was very hard for me. Time went on and finally, one day I got a call from her. She wanted to meet me, and I said, "Okay". She worked for Greyhound, and she had a meeting to see if she was going to take the job. I prayed that she did not.

I went to meet her for the first time since she left me. I was still hurt about everything she had done to me. Now, I was 5 years clean and had a nice car. I drove a 430 Lexus, had jewelry, looked good, and dressed very well. She had never seen me to this magnitude.

So, I got the chance to express myself just a little bit. I had made it up in my mind that she never loved me because she would have never in a million years done what she did. But even in my book, I'm not going to say what she did because God has changed my ways. It is not my place to say it ever. I know I could, but it's not my job to do so. They would have to.

Anyway, her and I met and had dinner at a restaurant in a hotel in downtown Minneapolis. We had drinks over dinner. She was trying to express her feelings. She wanted to go to bed with me and I said, "Do you think I'm a fool? After what you have done to me and my family, you think that I'm that weak to go to bed?"

I'm her Maudell, that was how she felt. But we were no longer lovers. I told her, "You take care of yourself and have a nice life". I got in my car and drove off.

At that point, I was still hurt but I knew how to control my feelings. I learned it from treatment. The treatment taught us girls how to live again through receiving the Lord Jesus, to get back into the word, and to live successfully. Thank God for my counselor. One of the best you'll ever meet.

I went to treatment by order of the court. I went for 28 days to in-patient treatment. It was hard but I was broken. Building myself back up, I learned to open up to people. I learned to be honest and to trust. I learned to be sober, and I learned to love people again. I learned to feel again. Treatment was the first step.

CHAPTER 5
Falling for the Wrong Guy

I MET A guy that worked at the Charlie Moon restaurant. He was so fine and lived down on 63rd Street in the high rise with his mom and sister. His mom was a single mom. He had his own room.

He went to Hyde Park High School. He was a sharp dresser and had long finger waves in his hair. He had a caramel complexion. He was all that and some more.

He would spend time with me, and I was pretty sharp myself. I thought we made a good couple. I loved him too. We went out and had fun with each other. I would meet him at his job, and we would go out.

I loved the way he made love to me. At this point, he was the best I ever had in bed. I love the way he treated me. I cared for his mom and his little sister and things were good. So, I cared for the family. We had a good life between the four of us. So, I thought it was very nice.

One day I was over at his house and the doorbell rang. It was his other woman, and she was pregnant by him. I was very hurt because I thought it was just me and him. I had no kids.

As time went on my feelings got more and more involved, until one day he said he was moving to California. I had never just jumped up and left my family, that was new for me. I did not know why this was happening so suddenly.

I was confused about what was going on. I was hurt. I felt sad and mad at the same time. I did not want him to leave. But my baby left me, and I was sad.

One day, I got a phone call letting me know that he had gotten stabbed. I don't know to this day if he is alive or dead. Where he is or if he has any kids? Maybe he's a lawyer? I just want to know where he is.

You know who you are. You know who I am. By the time I'm done with this book, you will be proud of me. May God keep you and your family. Love Maudell.

Gangster Love

Then I fell in love with a gangster. He was a very good person. I liked him from the start. He was a very good friend of my father. He was a straight hustler. He got paid big bucks, double-digit thousands.

He bought it to my attention, who I was. I was a drug dealer and a prostitute when I met him. I was out of drugs. I wanted to get a large packet and he was the only one who had some stuff. Someone took me to him, and I got nice sizes from him.

He said, "Who are you? You are getting your money. I like the way you carry yourself." He said, "If you come back you belong to me." He was a gangster and he had 8 bodyguards. When you walked in the door you got guns pulled on you, AKs, 9 mm, and 357 automatics, so he was well protected.

When I ran out of dope, I did not want to go back to him, but a customer was coming, and I needed to buy some more drugs. So, I went back to buy more, and he said you belong to me, and your name is Ms. Cadillac. The world needs to know who you belong to.

So, he took me with him. Me and all his bodyguards, and all his women. He was a gangster and big-time drug dealer and a pimp. He had lots of women and he got me set up. He was my man, and I was okay with it. He was so fine and handsome.

He took me to a hotel and had sex with me right away. Then he took me shopping and bought me clothes, and jewelry, and we bought cars. He sold kilos of dope and cocaine straight out of the keys.

He had 15 women, and they were his. But he put me away for 90 days because I was his number one and he let it be known. I started to have feelings for him, and he would serve people who did him wrong, or if anyone said or did anything to one of his girls or his folks, he was going off. Shooting and just straight killing people. Guns going bang. Guns were always going off.

Chapter 5
Falling for the Wrong Guy

We served off Pillsbury and Lake Street, Pleasant, Broadway, and Portland Park. He had the south and north sewed up. We would transport 10 keys at a time, and he rode with his boys. Riding day and night.

He would check on all his girls. He would have me out until 5:30 a.m. then we will go to our rooms. At that time, I was on drugs, and I was a moneymaker. The number one rule he had for me was not to get high until I'm done working.

So, I would go and transport his money and dope for him. He trusted me. I never took anything from him or lied to him. But if I got high, he would know if I was high. I could not talk because my throat was frozen.

The dope was pure. He didn't mix his dope because the people want to make a little money. They knew they could get some if the mix was good.

We would ride all over the city, back and forward, and all across the city. I was working Broadway, right off Broadway and Irving right on the corner. We had dope spots planted all over.

I spent a lot of time with his family. His uncle and cousins and his folks. So, now I am very much in love with him. But I noticed he would send this woman over where I was, and she would get thousands and thousands of dollars from me. Her name was Susan.

I always wondered who she was, but I knew she was my folk. We had the same man but that was it. He never opened up a lot about his life. I knew he was from Chicago, then lived in Minnesota, and his uncle, cousin, and his family. He continued to get women to work for him. He was always growing and growing, and we moved a lot of sex money, not just drug money.

He had people working everywhere and when they messed his money up, I hated to see what he did to them. Some could not walk, talk, or breathe, some people were shot. People have died all over, in alleys, in the garbage, in hallways, in cars, on the block, and on the sidewalk.

I was pulling them out of cars and beating them if his money wasn't right. So, I made sure it was or I was not going in until it was right. No sir. Yes, I was afraid of him. He was 6'8, 295lbs, steel solid, and ice-cold as could be.

Chapter 5
Falling for the Wrong Guy

That's when I met Wanda. She was a prostitute and a little-time dope dealer. We hung around Portland waiting for tricks day and night.

I would jump in and out of cars. I was making money like it was going out of style. I would rob men and take what I needed. I did not want to come up short. I was his bottom, so it had to be right. His money had to be right. At least on my behalf or he would be mad at me.

He did drugs and he was lots of fun. He had a right-hand man, and they would steal cars. Mercedes-Benz, Jaguars, Excaliburs, Lincolns, or Rolls-Royces. He moved any car in the world, but he was a violent person.

He was a lover and I cared for him. I would go down to his house and cook, play cards, drink, and have fun with his friends, his girlfriend, and other people. He was the best in bed. I loved the way he made love to me.

He would lick me from my ears, down to my breast, and all down in between my legs, down to my toe, and back up to my shoulders. In and out, everywhere up and down and down and around and back to my breasts and back down between my legs.

It was in and out until I would not breathe. Over and over, again and again. Then we would sleep and eat. I would have oral sex with him, kissing him from his head to his toes. We would have sex until we were drained. We would rest and get high over and over.

So, Dad was the dope man, and he was a man of his word. I was not worried about drugs. Whatever he wanted he got. I miss him. Dad, I wonder where you are. Are you alive, and okay? He was my sex machine, and I was his sex machine.

As long as he was working, he would spend time with me, giving me what I asked for. Too bad it had to end, but life must go on. It was good while it lasted. All is well, baby.

It was good until he started hitting me. I was getting high and that was a no-no. I could not see that or what he meant, but I'm sure it was for my own good.

Every night he made sure when he slept, it was with me. He would pick me up, take me off from everyone else to beat me or to make love and he would do it so hard until I would cry and be sore. But I went no matter what. I needed to do what I needed to do to make his money right.

I did not know anything but him. Things got bad. The beatings day in and day out. Eyes getting black, nose bust, and lips messed up. I think he wanted to beat women, as I was not the only one. There were lots of times he would let me serve them. I was a gangster. I was not a punk to no other. Maybe him but not to anyone else.

So that's the way it was. He was not right at all. Now my feelings are getting very cold, so now I wanted to kill him and everyone else because this was not right. He would treat me so cold that I thought the day would come when he would kill me with his own hands. My heart was cold. I was bitter. I had hate in my heart.

I had taken this dope dealer off. It was a lot of money, dope, and guns. That was one of the bigger moves I had ever made with him. I called him to come and get me. I told him I was at the Fair Oaks Hotel. He knew the corners I worked. He would go past and not see me and he would wonder where I was and why I'm calling him.

My mother, my sister, and my family did love me, and I knew they did but sometimes it didn't feel like they did. I always was different. I was cracked very bad. I needed help but just did not know how to get it. He kept me medicated all the time. He did not want me to get help.

Then I started thinking about things I never thought of before. It seemed just like God had opened my eyes, so I could see something I had never seen before. The real was being shown to me. I thank God but I knew I had a long way to go.

People wanted to kill me because I was with him and what he represented and who he was. So, Melvin don't like me or him, they wanted me dead, but God said, "No, get away from him".

I made up my mind, I was out of Minnesota. They can have the whole state. But he sent someone in the crack house to see if I was in there and told me it was a rich white man that had a lot of money, so I took a hit of the pipe and threw it to the sidewall, ran outside, jumped in a car and it was a Cadillac.

Women were in the car. He drove me to Wisconsin and said for me to get out of the car and teach the girls how to work a truck stop. I got on a CB to show her how to turn a date and how to get a date. We made so much money.

I ended up going to jail and he left me in jail. So that let me know right then and there that this man did not care for me. I never thought he did. They kept me in jail until I went to court. When they let me out, I found a way back to Minnesota only by God's grace and mercy.

When I saw him again, I was on Portland, and he was in the car driving. He had Lola in the car, and he got very mad. He said, "Get in". I didn't. He said, "You will wish that you had got in" and he said, "Are you sure" and I said, "Yes" and he drove off.

I walked across the street and 13 guys came up to me and kick me in my chest and kick me and beat me until blood was all over me and I was messed up. Very, very bad, and I just laid there until they thought that they killed me. When they left and I continued to lay there.

But God led me there and carried me home. When I got to the door, I rang the doorbell and my dad answered and I fell in his arms. They called the police and the ambulance, and I went to the hospital. I had been beaten badly and I was hurt.

I felt betrayed and bitter, and hate was in my heart. I wanted to kill everyone, but I took a turn for the worst in ICU. I was on my deathbed. I didn't think that I would make it, but God was on my side, and I went into a coma. Police were always at my door because it was gang related. My brother and my family were there, and they were very, very, upset about what happened.

They were questioning me about what happened, but I did not say anything to them because I was going to personally take care of it. He didn't care to see me so that is when I knew he did this to me. Anytime someone put their hands on me or said anything to me, he would beat them down or have them shot. So, I knew he had done this.

I was in the hospital for three months. God gave me the strength to walk. I knew he bought me through this. I have always known who God was since I was a little girl. So, I stayed there until I was completely well. Before I got out of there, people were shot and killed.

Then people knew who my folks were, and other people knew. When I got out, I did not look back.

I went home and talked to my family, and I decided to leave town because it was a hot mess all around me. People were getting killed in hotels and cars, in the streets, and everywhere I turned. So, I knew if I did not leave someone was going to kill me or I was going to kill someone.

That's when I Matthew. The owner of the apartment on Lake Street. He gave me a place to live, and he took care of me. He bought me food and gave me a job in his store. He had a t-shirt shop. Me and another girl I knew worked there, and CK. I met his wife and got on my feet. He and I had sex. Then I left town and never looked back.

Benton Harbor Michigan Jail

I went to jail for an unarmed robbery. I was messed up on crack cocaine and my habit was very bad. I would do just about anything to get my next high. I was not playing about getting my money.

One day, I robbed a retired police officer and did not know he was a retired police officer because he did not have on a uniform. I took his money out of his pocket and ran. He did not chase me because he was in the hood. He didn't because of what would have happened. I'm glad he did not put up a fight or anything.

So, I went about my business, and later that week, I robbed this nurse in the same hood. I always got people on my ground.

I was at home when the doorbell rang and my husband was in the bed. He got up and answer the door and when he opened the door, they push their way in, flashed the light on me, and arrested me.

I was naked. They let me put on my clothes and my husband said, "Please, let her put on a coat?" They took me down and they came and identified me. They said, "It's her". I was sentenced to 8 months in St Joseph County Jail.

O' My God

I got a job on the work crew. Me and five other women all had our own space. One day, we were on the road. Working on the highway and it was my turn to ride with the sheriff. The sheriff had a gun.

So, a woman on the crew Beth-Anne or Beth said to me, "Please let me get in the front today. I know it is your turn to but let me sit up there". I said, "Is it that serious?" So, I said, "Okay". But remind you she had not been acting herself. So, I was thinking about that but paid no attention to it.

She got in and something happened. Oh my God is all I could think. When I look up and saw she had taken the police gun. This cannot be happening to us. Oh my, what is going on?

I looked in the mirror and gave her that look like you are trained for this here. So, I'm still looking, and I put my hand back to the cage to see if I could fit. So, she went for her gun to get it back from her. They start wrestling over the gun and she grabbed her hair very hard so she can get her gun back because when we pull up, we saw bags. We thought she had planned something.

She went running away from us. By now, police from all over are on the scene. It was the craziest thing that I had ever seen before. It was crazy because she only had 90 days. She was in there for larceny. She had been on crack for one year. I was on crack for 10 years or more, had a robbery case, and was black. She was white. So, this was very surprising to the city and everyone who heard about it.

Her boyfriend had gone to prison for a very long time. He had written a letter telling her how to escape and when to do it and everything. He told them everything they wanted to know. He told them when she was at the hotel.

So, they went back to where she was at. When they got to the hotel and went in, she was naked and laid out on the bed. They came into the room, got her, and took her back to jail where we were.

So, the big boss said, "Who is Hardison-Hadley?" I said, "I am". He said, "Words cannot express how I feel? How can I ever say thank you. You will get something for this. I don't know what it is yet".

He said, "What would you like to eat, whatever you want to do?" I said, "McDonald's, a Big Mac, something for all of us, and some Newport's" that is what they wanted, and some chewing gum. He got us what we wanted.

We went back to the jail, and they told us what happened. They went to his job, her boyfriend, and they demanded he tell them where she was, or he was going to go to jail.

Beth ended up getting 38 years. That was so sad. They ended up giving me 42 days of credit for saving everyone's life, including my own. They took the 5 years' probation from it and that was just good for me. I was grateful for what God had done in our lives because one thing I know, if nothing else, God is in control. He's working things out.

We were on TV, in the newspaper, and everything. So, I knew God was always there with me and for me. I thank God for everything he has allowed me to go through. Even my bad choices. I thank him for everything and his Son, Jesus Christ, the Lord. Amen.

In the Mental Ward

Well, I remember being in the mental ward. I was suicidal, depressed, sad, mad, hurt, bitter, and angry. I felt like the world was against me and I was prepared to die any day. For that reason, I needed to stay there. My husband at the time thought that it would be the right thing to do. So, I said, "Ok" and I went, and I was admitted.

A couple of people there were in bad shape too. I talked to the head doctor, and he gave me my meds. I was medicated all the time. I don't remember how long but I do remember asking to take my life because I knew God at the age of five. That was all Mom Dear talked about, so it was normal for me.

As I look back now, I can see in the realm of the spirit, how Satan tried to take my life. God said, "You can touch her but not kill her. I'm going to use this for my glory." So, depression, sadness, anger, bitterness, and thoughts of suicide had to go in the name of Jesus.

Demons had to flee in the name of Jesus. Satan was trying to kill me when I was born. My mom's umbilical cord had wrapped around my neck, and she had five minutes to have me, or we would have died.

When I think back over my life, it reminds me a lot of Job in the bible. Not to compare my life with Job's because that would be foolish. Job's life and my life are very different. But it was the same devil. Through it all I had faith for more than 44 years that I have the same mindset about Jesus, the Lord and who they were, and the Holy Ghost. The Holy Spirit is the action, and I was always told all three are one.

Chapter 5
Falling for the Wrong Guy

But I was so sad and lonely. I did try to overdose to kill myself, but God said, "No". I did not understand what was going on, but I found out that God had a purpose for my life. I was ordained by God and handpicked by God and anointed by the Holy One.

As I write, the Holy Spirit is moving this morning. We must thank God first and foremost, that he has a plan for our lives. As I continue to read His word, to learn about the Holy Bible and the Holy Ghost, he began to show me the hidden mystery in the word of God because it was only for his people.

CHAPTER 6
My Kids

WHEN I HAD my first child, I loved her very much. She was so special. It is something about the firstborn. It is something different. You cannot put your hands on it. She was born on May 26, 1982.

When she was born, she had lots of problems like her brain was not complete. Her little body was only 4 lbs. and 3 oz. She was very tiny, and she looked like her dad.

She lived for only five days. The day she died was the saddest day of my life. I was so hurt. I felt like I had nothing to live for. My life was upside down. I never knew she was going to die, and I felt like I could have saved her. She was my baby, and I was so sad.

I will never forget the day we got her dressed in pink for the funeral. I bought her coffin clothes and flowers. I did my best as a mom should have done. My life took a turn for the worst. I didn't want to live.

I so hated God for sure for taking her from me. I did not understand why. So, I wanted to kill myself. I was very suicidal, and I shut everyone out of my life because she was my only life. I loved my baby with everything I had in me.

After this, the Army called him in. You know how that goes. He blamed me for everything, but it was not my fault that God took her from us. Things happen in life that are not fair and as I'm writing this book, this happened more than 28 years ago, and it still hurts very bad. But God said if I release this, he will heal me completely. I know his word is true and I trust him with everything.

Today, even though she is gone, I know she is in Heaven with God. She is here in the spirit. This is very difficult to write but the truth must come for healing to take place. So, one day her daddy would know the truth and forgive me.

I went into the mental ward behind this. Not knowing how to deal with life. Mom loves you, and we dedicate this book to your daddy, until we meet again.

My second child was born on May 15, 1985. She weighed 8 lbs. and 6 oz. She was a very beautiful daughter and I loved her more than life.

My mom raised her because I was on crack cocaine very bad. I had her for three years before my life crashed. So, I tried to do what was right for my child to be safe. I can imagine how she felt, longing for her mom's love. I had a very hard life, but I love my daughters. No matter what happened, I would give my life for my girls' life.

Now, my daughter loved her daddy, but he died of a heart attack. We miss him. I was married to him for five years. We both were remarried so we had a good life. She was a very good daughter. I would powder her up and dress her in PJs. She would sleep all night long. My baby was good.

She is my special sweetheart. She is my princess. I started getting high at the age of 23. So, by this time I was so far gone on crack cocaine and faded away, it was so bad that I hate myself.

But I wanted to do what was best for her. So, my mother had her at first. But my mom worked, so she asked Lola to keep her. I knew her so I was okay with her.

My baby was 6 lbs. 4 oz, and I didn't think my baby was going to weigh that much because I was getting high the whole time I was carrying her. My sister took her at 2 weeks old and raised her. Her and her husband. As time went on and on, I continued to work the street and get high. Doing my thing. They raised my daughter.

She is a beautiful girl. Now she is a young lady. At the time I was writing this, she was 18 years old. So, I said to my daughter, "I did what was best for you and you were a soloist in the world. I hate myself for this, but God is in my life today. He is my life and no matter what you have heard, this book is the truth about my life. It is not good, but it is for God's glory. So read and understand that's what it was."

Chapter 6
My Kids

My daughter understands what I went through. So, she forgives me and today my daughter is a prophetess, her husband is a minister, and she has two daughters and a son. Her father-in-law is the pastor of their church.

As I sit here and write, only two men come to mind, Stanley Christian and Malcomb Ross who could be her father, because when she was born, she was white with blue eyes. One of the men that comes to mind has eyes just like that. He was married so I repent for that. We were together for a long time. He was my pimp, that's what it was.

I love my daughter and ask her forgiveness for not knowing who her father was from day one. I was so messed up that I did not know when my birthday was. I would pass by people celebrating the Fourth of July, so I knew my birthday was on the 16th of that month.

Sometimes I would be so messed up that I would not know anything. I was 90 lbs., my eyes were so black under them, and I was just ashamed of myself. So, I would not go around my family. Most of the time, I would just keep to myself. I just kept away from them so I would not have to feel so ashamed about my life.

I know this without a doubt, I love my children, including my son whom I lost by miscarriage. In all, I have three girls and one boy.

At this time, I have two daughters that are living, so I felt God only wanted me to have two girls. I plan on having a chance to bond with my children again, this is what my heart desires more than ever. To have my two boys playing together, doing everything together.

I do have a grandson. But my daughter has been told so many lies about me. So, God has set the record straight once and for all. At the time I was writing this book, I just have a strong bond with one of my daughters that I would like to have with my baby.

She's so sweet. She's grounded. At the time I was writing this book, she had been working for 3 years and is in her first year of college majoring in criminal justice. I just feel like me and her need to spend more time together. After reading this book she can give me my first interview with both of my daughters. I'm ready for the world, so I am asking my daughter to please forgive me. I did what I thought was best.

To God be the glory. I hope you won't be ashamed of telling your friends I'm your mother. Don't wait until I'm dead to say how you really feel. I'm a big girl. I can handle anything through Christ Jesus that strengthens me.

CHAPTER 7
Sugar Daddies

I MET THIS man while dancing in Storm Lake Iowa. He would always come in on the weekend. All the girls would be all over him, so I watched and kept making money. Brandy was it at that time and it was lots of fun. We all got along together, and we danced from Monday through Saturday. I made about 6 to 7 thousand a week at that place. But everywhere is different.

I was on the stage, and I dressed very classy. I had on lace, feather, silk diamonds on every hand, and 6-

inch heels. I had the clothes I would wear every day. I changed 3 to 4 times a day.

One day, a man walked into the place. He's got on dirty clothes, and boots, and smelled very bad. He asked me for a dance. I looked and he asked me for a date. He had $200 and for some reason I did it. But when I date someone, I always get more money.

He was waiting for me to change out of my clothes. We left, wrote a check, and cashed it. He was a farmer, and I went to his farm. We did not have sex or anything. He was over 40 years old. He was very lonely, and we talked.

He had all kinds of land and just one tractor worth over $250,000. He was worth $10 million, and his daddy was worth $35 million. He said, "How much do you make a week?" I said, "6, 7, 10 thousand". He said, "I will give you $10,000 to hold with me and work with him on the farm. That Saturday he did, and I went home. I kept in touch with him.

I met his dad and he fell in love with me. He liked me a lot, but that mother was not having it. But dad overruled her. However, she was his accountant and every dime he spent, she knew everything. She was down with meeting me, but there was just one problem. I was black. She hated that. So prejudiced, but she did not control him. Not yet.

So, he was giving me money left and right. He gave me $30,000 and he let me borrow $30,000 and a little more, and mom hit the roof. When I went to cash the check, the people looked at me like I had killed someone. You know they were thinking that I had stolen a check.

They called him and he came up there. He said, "What's the problem?" They said, "Is the amount right on that check?" He said, "Yes, cash it now". When they cashed my check, I got the money, put it in the trunk of my car, and went to work on the farm.

I was a farm girl. Born and raised in Helena, Arkansas, and raised on a farm. He taught me how to give shots to the pigs, clip tails, and wash the pigs' houses down. He taught me how to dress on the farm, he taught me to work the combo, and how to bell hay. We built a shed for the pigs and kept them safe until one day she threatened him, that he was losing his mind because of the things he was doing for me.

She put him in a mental hospital and said he was crazy. She took over his money so he could not spend another dime on me. So, I promise my mom on her deathbed that I would pay him the $30,000 back, just to show his mom that he was right, and she was wrong.

So, he told me that she was scared for me, and it was not safe on the farm anymore. So, I went on a dance with Riley. I was in Carol Iowa dancing for the week. It was Christmas time, and I was supposed to fly out a day before Christmas. It was storming and everything was shut down. Stores, even the airport. No flights were flying out.

I was so upset and called Bryan and told him and he said, "I'm coming to get you, Mercedes," I said, "You're going to die because it is storming". He said, "I know the back road. I am on my way. Ok, I'm coming".

He came and picked me up and we went to have dinner. He gave me a cell phone, a diamond ring, and $5,000. He said he liked me, come go out. I said, "Yes". Then he bought another ring. It was 2,000 carats and he got me a jewelry card with a $70,000 credit line with my name on the card. Then we went to Minnesota to get a room and it was on.

Here Comes Another Sugar Daddy

Every week he was there. Everywhere I danced he was there. At that time, I had about 10 sugar daddies and 50 tricks. I was in Denison, Iowa. I got a call, and I did not know who it was. I got on the phone and said, "Hello, this is Mercedes".

He said, I know you don't know who I am, but this is my birthday, and I want to spend it with you. Don't worry about money, I have it. See you soon.

So, I was on stage dancing to bad to the bone, in cowgirl clothes. All black boots. He said, "Hello Mercedes" and started to throw $20, and $100 bills all over the stage. I always needed a Ziploc to pick up my money.

On this night this man said he wanted to give me a gift and I said, "Okay" and he wrote me a check for $3,000 and asked her who this girl was, and she said, "You are fired". I said, "Whatever". He asked what was wrong. I told him what happened.

When I left with any man, he had to meet me there, and give me a down payment. When we got that it was good. I had him and other men in different rooms. So, the guy was so upset about me being fired, he wrote me another check for $13,000 and took me to his bank.

A Quick Message for the Ladies

One of my sugar daddies gave me $4,000 and said I need a truck in 5 days. He bought a truck for $30,000 and gave me $7,000 in cash and went on the job to get me. He was married so that was not good at all but I'm a hooker, so what about her.

I always felt that a woman should take care of her husband or man in every way, so they don't have to cheat. Having dated a lot of married men, I have asked all my clients, why they cheat, and this was the response. My wife doesn't like sex, or she doesn't go down on me. That was in the brothels in Nevada.

The most men I have had in one day is 50 so you have a good idea of what I'm saying. I have interviewed at least 3,000 men and they all said the same thing. I said, "Wow, if these women only knew what the problem really is and why some husbands leave their wives for a hooker!" Some are getting divorced because the woman in the brothel listened.

Chapter 7
Sugar Daddies

Please, your husbands care for each of you and your kids, and will do anything in the world with you, why can't you go down on your husband? You are one. Whatever you do you cannot be held accountable because in God's eyes you are one. Get this or you will not have a husband in the long run. Catch this just like you some sexual satisfaction from him, he deserves that same treatment or better than what he does to you.

If you don't keep your fire burning it will go out. So, feel me, ladies? I want to see you happy that is why I am putting this out there. You don't have to like what I'm saying but please, with all due respect, please hear me. I'm on your side because God changed my life. This was when I was of the world. Don't get it twisted.

Charles fell in love with me because he was married, he said he did not want to have sex with his wife. First of all, she is too fat, doesn't like sex, and just likes to spend money when she wants to. Second, he likes chocolate.

So, the story is she found out about us, and she called the cell phone saying that they need the truck back and I was a nigger. I told her, "Where do you need to meet? At what highway because if you have sex with him, get your white you know what, and do something with him, so he will not spend $37,000.

Some men just love to have variety. 98% of women, I feel, play a bigger part than they know, but I live it. So, I do know from experience, and for me, I was of the world doing whatever I wanted to do. I chose to be a prostitute and that's what I did for a living. They came to me.

But today, I hurt writing this. I put myself in your shoes and I don't like the way it feels. Yes, I always had safe sex, even when I went down on them. So, love me first and look out for our lives. To God be the glory for Charles.

For my sugar daddy, his wife was out of line for calling me. She should have asked him why or what was that all about. So, I don't get into it. That was between him and his wife because I don't know if they had a fight or if they are getting a divorce. I don't know and it is not my business.

So, for this couple, it's one of the saddest things that ever could happen to anyone. He no longer wanted to be with his wife, and he wanted out of the marriage. He could not have me, so they say that he killed himself. They said he put the gun to his head and blew his brains out.

I don't believe that for one second and it is more to that than what they are saying. I pray to God that the truth is uncovered, please in the name of Jesus.

Back to My Latest Sugar Daddy

I went to Walmart with Charles and some others. We were looking for a TV. All of a sudden, this man passed by and said, "Hi. What kind of TV are you guys looking for?" I looked at my boyfriend and the others with me.

He just kept right on looking, then he passed by again and said, "Hello, what's your name?" I said, "Mercedes". He said, he's Joseph. He then asked, "What do you do?" I said, "I'm an investor". He then asked, "What do you do" and I said, "I'm an investor in guns". I looked at Charles, he looked at me.

Then the man gave me a card. He gave me a business card and took me out to Red Lobster. I pulled up in my gold s type V850 Jaguar bought at the Land Rover car lot. We had a very nice time. He was a gentleman. He had a real chauffeur's license, and we went to buy me a Chrysler, white and black, Chrysler woodgrain 2009. He also got me a Mercedes E320, black on black, very beautiful and very fast.

So, John start liking me, but he was a Jehovah's witness and that was a big problem for me. I just don't believe in that, I believe in the Father, Son, and Holy Spirit, all three are one. I believe in the Trinity, and I was raised Baptist but I'm not Baptist anymore. I'm non-denominational. It is about Christ Jesus.

He tried to teach me and show me what he believed. But he and I could not see eye to eye when it came to who we serve. From there, everything went downhill, and he left, and I never saw him again.

Here Comes Another One

So, let's talk about Mr. Newman. I went to Austin to Hey Ruby, that's what it used to be before Ruby died. I went down there with a person named Natalie. I met Mr. Newman when he came in. He and I talked. He wanted to go with me back to Minnesota. I said let's go to the Mystic Lake Casino. Back then I lived in New Prague Minnesota. He tried to cash a check, but something happened, but anyway, we went shopping.

He bought me a John Deere, a big one, that cost $2,500 and bought me a little pull one, and then he bought a big grill for $2,000. Then he got me a jewelry card and he bought me a CLK430 convertible, all black, Mercedes-Benz. Then he got me 24 credit cards.

Mr. Newman was getting a divorce from his wife, so he was very lonely, sad, and hurt. I couldn't see any of this at first, so we had a very good time. I slept with him one time.

My car got stolen. When they found it, he called me to say the police found it. I'm going to get it back. I said, "God has changed my life, so keep the car because that is what the Holy Spirit said to me."

I know God was changing my life. I felt different. I started thinking differently.

He was not supposed to go near his and his wife's home. She had a restraining order against him. But he kept going there and he got arrested. I found out and I went to see him, and I never saw him again.

Wait, There's More…

I met Charles J from prison through his ex-wife. I want to say first and foremost, I asked for forgiveness for leading him wrong. I was still of the world, I had to have everything that I came across, but I truly had Satan working inside of me. I allowed him. So, for that reason please forgive me. Thank God that I can say that with my whole heart, amen.

After that, I met James in Vegas on Fremont Street, in the hood of Las Vegas. The low end. I met him and we moved so much money it was unreal. He went to Iowa to pick up my money and never returned.

So, I don't know what happened. We moved over half a million dollars. It was good. For a sugar daddy in Wisconsin, he was so good to me.

My sugar daddy in Wisconsin took very good care of me. He bought me $8,000 of lingerie and he paid for my room in the sex house. He paid for one month and he gave me $2,000 a week and 25 more. So, it was very good money. He cared for me for years.

Well, Dexter, I met him at the Lady Luck in Spencer Iowa. He was hard to get. They said I could not get any money out of him. It took me one week to get $23,000 from him. He was a trip around the world. He was very different. He really was not a fool, but he did get tricked because he set himself up.

If that's not enough, I met another man named Dexter in Des Moines, Iowa at Motel 6. I was coming out of my hotel room going to get some food. I had run out of gas, so he said, "Hi. How are you doing and where have you been.? So, I'm looking at him like, what are you talking about?

He thought he knew me, but he really did not, but you cannot tell him that. He said he owes me money. A million dollars. I said, "What" to myself. I went down to see what was going to become of this.

So, he went to get gas and went to Minnesota with me and spent over $30,000 like it was water. He spent so much money. I called him, a Million Dollar Man. He was loving every bit of it. So unreal, but so real. He got me a condo furnished with everything. It was my own until my Million Dollar Man got nervous.

He said he knew my boyfriend. He said they went to college together and he tried to take his girlfriend. That's what he said to my man. So, my man said he was crazy and felt like he must have tried something when we were sleeping.

Yes, he was in my condo. I felt it was the right thing to do when someone is that good to you. So, I took him downtown and that was the end of that.

CHAPTER 8
Here Comes the Bride

IN 1998, Bryan and I got married. We went to the courthouse and got married, and afterward had a very big wedding reception. It was very nice. I had on a beautiful black gown, and he had on a very nice black suit. Lots of food, drinking, and dancing. I dance in Sussex, Iowa, and that's where I got married.

To my surprise, the DJ announced that I was getting married. At that time, I had at least 26 sugar daddies or more and I did not know that Bryan had told anyone in the bar we were going to get married.

When it came over the loudspeaker, as I was on stage dancing, I heard it and I saw some of my sugar daddies that heard it leave the bar. I had a big-time farmer leave. We had been dating for a long time and he would bring thousands there just for me.

I never said anything because he had been the top one of all time. He would do anything for me, and I mean anything as long as it was not breaking the law. Bryan has never been in trouble. I lived a life in which that's all that happened was me breaking the law and doing whatever I wanted. It was just crazy.

So, time went on and he signed for my boyfriend a two-bedroom condo and he bought me a big diamond ring. I could get anything I wanted anywhere. He was in construction and so he made very good money. He had very good credit. For Mother's Day, he bought me an 18-ft Sea Ray, blue and white, brand new, and he bought a drop-top convertible.

These are the things he gave me. He has given me millions of dollars and he has bought me millions of dollars in just jewelry, work clothes, shoes, and my condo. Always laid out from top to bottom. I lived in the best areas, and he stayed with me everywhere I would go. At every dance place, he would put thousands of dollars on the stage. He loved me and I knew it. So, when the word got out that he married me, now the girls wanted to test him and see what he would do. But I had it sewed up.

I was very serious about everything that I did with any tricks because I knew how the game went. It is what it is. So, I knew he was tricked whenever I met him, and he will be tricked when I leave him. Nothing lasts forever, so I wanted to get what I can and move on. That's the way the game goes.

So, he was not allowed to answer my phone, my door, or ask me any questions, even though he was giving me millions, his money was not long enough. No man's money would measure for what I'm really worth because even then I knew who I belonged to.

I have always belonged to the true and living God but just did not know how to come to him. One reason is that I was sinning so much until I was afraid of myself.

Bryan would come to Minnesota, we lived off Brooklyn Center so when he come to where I lived, he would have to wait until I came out. He was not allowed to come to the door. So, my man was okay with the decision that I made.

I could be cold as ice, but I was serious about my life, my kids, and my family. My kids were off-limits to any man I came in contact with because if a man touch one of my children, I can guarantee you I would kill them for sure, go to prison, and do my time. So, for that alone, they were off-limits. I thank God that he never allowed anything to happen to my children and that they are grown women today. Married and have their own families.

At that time, my youngest daughter was in college and working and had a boyfriend. I prayed he would give his life 100% to the true and living God so God can mold him into the man He called him to be. God bless my son-in-law.

So, life went on with me and my husband. Only one time did he support me in prison. I had money, so half of the time he did not know what was going on with me. It would get to the point where I start playing checks and it was very sweet until I got a 10-year sentence to go to Mitchellville Iowa prison.

Chapter 8
Here Comes the Bride

Life was not looking too good. But that did not stop me, I kept doing silly stuff, not even thinking. Just whatever I did was right to me, and you know why? Because I was blind. Even though I had eyes to see. I was deaf even though I had ears to hear.

I had been off drugs for at least 9 years at that time, so no deal at all. He bought a $500,000 home and he bought me three buildings so I can rent them out. He bought me 12 cars. He ended up buying 3.11 million of property. So, this was the end of our life together.

I went to prison in 2004, for failure to appear. I tried to stay out as long as I could. I never told my husband about it, so when I got arrested for 7 months, I did not talk to him. He let his family talk him into divorcing me. When he found out that I was in prison, the sheriff came to the door, and they got me.

When I got in the room and saw who it was, I took the paper, smiled, and went back to my unit and called him. When he found out that I was there, he said he loved me and don't sign it. I said, "If you had the nerve to send it to me, then I have enough nerve to sign it."

So, we will see. I prayed and asked God to show me something because I wanted to do the right thing because he has been very good to me. I didn't want to do something that would hurt me in the long run. I got to follow Jesus.

One day, I received a letter from my sister, and I tell you it was from God. So, I signed the paper and sent them to the lawyer, and I got a divorce on August 18, 2008. My husband and I were done. Sex was cut off like 2 years before. I gave God my life 100% but had lots of things that I had done.

So, I had a price to pay back for what I had done. Lots of wrong things. I had to pay by going to prison. In jail, I had a level 6 score on my criminal history. It was not good, but I was okay with it.

So, today I live only for God. By the way, at that time I was in jail for an $85 bad check. I had been in there for 55 days by the time I went to court. I'm a minister and I knew I would someday be writing this book about my life and how God changed my life.

Everyone in the Bible went through, and so shall we. But God is always with us no matter what we go through. We belong to him. People may beat us down physically, but our souls belong to God and that is something I'm not willing to lose. I have given everything that I had but not my soul. I thank Him for delivering me from every evil spirit that I had that was not of him but from Satan.

I worked for Satan for a long time but today I belong only to God. I am married to God in the spirit but waiting on my husband in the natural, amen. I've been back to prison and in jail and taken away from my family. I have been hit but you know what, I can make it.

I can do anything through Christ Jesus that strengthens me. I will prevail. No weapon formed against me shall prosper. I do know this, God has me, no matter what I go through, how long I'm in jail, or in hell, Jesus went to hell to get me and for his Father's glory. I AM who I AM sent me. He sent His Son, so He is sending me, amen.

Teaching Others the Game

There was a guy that knew my sister's baby daddy, DAX. He was a manager for his records. He was talking to me, and I liked him from the very start. He was a crip and I liked him because he was straight to the point. He said, "I'm not a pimp but I know you are a real "b", and you get your money."

Please show me how it goes, pimping, and everything there is to know about the game. Every in and out. He was with the best so we can do nothing but go up. He said, "I don't know anything about it, so teach me. I'm willing to learn."

We had something to do first. I had a bad drug habit, so I lied to go to treatment for 28 days. He was there for me. I got out and I went to dance in Storm Lake Iowa, and I danced there for a week. We went to Denison, Iowa for a week. We went to Fremont, Nebraska for a week. We went to Austin, Minnesota for a week. We went to Green Bay, Wisconsin.

Then we went to North Dakota for a week. I went to Eagle Grove for a week, I went to Spencer, Iowa for a week. I went to Holgred, Nebraska for 2 weeks. I went to Yankton, South Dakota for a week, I went to Keene, Nebraska for a week. I went to Estherville for a week. I went to Black River Falls for a week. I went to Cumberland, Wisconsin for a week. I went to Dutch, Minnesota for a week. I went to Sioux Fall for a week. I went to Marsh Town Iowa for a week. I went to 38 states.

Chapter 8
Here Comes the Bride

He and I lived out of hotels and motels when we traveled. We did that for some time. As time went on, he and I had a conversation about sex houses somewhere in Nevada. He had a close friend, and his friend had a girl down there working while I was back in Green Bay dancing for the week.

I noticed my man had not called or come to the place where I was, but I was not worried. I wondered where he was or if he was okay. So, I just kept on working and stacking thousands of dollars until he walked in on his last day.

On Saturday night he explained where he was and what he had been doing. He was out of town with his friends in Elko, Nevada. He went on and on saying, "Baby I went to these sex houses, JP, Sue, Manola, and Mona too, and Inez. There are hundreds of thousands of dollars to be made. So, I said, "Let's do it, baby, because I love you and what to be with you for the rest of my life."

We talked and talked more and spent all of our time together. If you saw him, you see me. He was my baby. We sat down and talked and talked and got our game plan down packed. We agreed that no man could ever come into my life. So that I would be faithful, loyal, open, and understanding and he would do the same. He would not cheat.

Being a call girl, I would always use safe sex, and I wouldn't bring him any disease. So, please tell the truth. We both agreed and then we talked about life. I asked what he wanted out of life, and he asked me what I wanted.

I would like to have a big, beautiful home. I would like for you to have a nice car and truck. I would like for me to have a very nice car and a truck. A big, nice boat and very nice furniture from room to room, and everything in the whole house completely matching.

I would like to have nice and expensive jewelry, our food stocked up, and at least $10,000 cash on hand at all times. A very small, nice little dog for me, and your son and for him to have anything our kids wanted.

I wanted to have money in the bank. I wanted to be able to trust him with my life. I wanted to travel, and have very nice expensive clothes, and shoes, shop at Saks Fifth, Victoria's Secret, Macy's, Neiman Marcus, Gucci, Versace, Silk lingerie lace, and shoes.

Chapter 8
Here Comes the Bride

In the work I do, I have to look like a million to make millions.

I have very high maintenance and he had to allow me to spend lots of money and buy big black diamonds, so we had to get an understanding of everything because I knew what was going to happen because I knew me. I have to say I was a cold piece.

I wanted him and I to experience everything, having everything we had, but all things together. Open a business than just blow up over the years. Be married and be happy for the rest of our lives. So, we want the same things out of life.

We agreed to start to get things together. I lived in Minneapolis, Minnesota at that time and I called my sugar daddy to say that I need to use his credit cards. He said, "Come here, baby. I will be here. Wait, I want to hear about everything you are trying to do". I said, "Okay sweetheart."

So, we went to Wisconsin, told my man what was going on, and what he said. So, he said, "Okay baby". I took off and went there. I cleaned his house as we were talking about me going to work at this sex house where I can make lots of money. $3,000 to $6,000 a night. He said to call and order my lingerie, lace, silk, shoes, gown, and dresses.

He spent $8,000 on clothes. That did not include play toys, condoms, etc. We also called to pay for my room and board in Elko, Nevada, before I even got there, and I got myself a room to stay in while I get ready.

When I got off the phone, I spent some time with my sugar daddy. He just likes to lay in bed to cuddle. He's 78 years old, and I was only 32 years old at that time. He was a very nice guy. I had him and 19 more. I had 20 sugar daddies that took very good care of me.

So, I'm on my way back to Minneapolis, Minnesota, me, and my man. At this time, I was married to my top sugar daddy. He took care of me. He bought me diamonds, cars, and clothes, he gave me $3,000 a week from him and he gave me $30,000. Anytime I needed money he would loan big loans. He met me anywhere when he needed to see me. He bought me cell phones and anything I wanted.

I had sugar daddies in Salt Lake, New York, New Jersey, LA, California, Montana, Idaho, Chicago, Wisconsin, Iowa, Texas, Canada, Rochester,

Chapter 8
Here Comes the Bride

Maryland, Boston, Baltimore, Minnesota, Las Vegas, Reno Nevada, Lake Tahoe, Dutch Minnesota, Lake Superior, Hudson Wisconsin, London England, Japan, and China. I had men jump out of airplanes to come to see.

In 1995, I got together with one of my other sugar daddies. Everything was so good. My main sugar daddy would come in and out of the bar. Girls all over him. He saw me and asked me out and we went to go on a date, and it was no return. He gave me table dances, and private dances, and when we went out, he paid well.

But, as I said, I was already with someone else, before my main sugar daddy came into my life, so I was not going to let no trick come between us, what we had, and what we were trying to build. It was an empire I was building. A very big and tall empire.

I let every trick know I'm in control of my life and the decisions I made. So, that they would be gone so fast that they try to control my life that was not going to happen. Not in my life.

So, he and I are getting ready to go to Elko, Nevada for the first time. We are taking off now. We are on our way to the airport to fly from Minnesota to Salt Lake City and change planes to go to Elko. Delta Airlines is the only one that goes to Elko, a very small town.

We got there, me and my man. He said that he would not leave me until he knows that everything was good. So, he went to the hotel until I let him know what was going on.

I had someone take me to the doctor and from the doctor to the police station to be legal in Nevada for prostitution. I stayed with my man for a couple of days, then I went to the house to start work.

My first paycheck was $9,000 and that was $50 for 5 minutes. So, by the time you would check clean, got a condom, and got it in it was time to pay again. So, you have to be very convenient to get $5,000 and up and I had become very convenient, very persuading, and confident at what I was doing.

I stayed there for 2 to 3 months at a time. I was trying to make millions. I needed to be there like it was my home away from home. I missed my kids, my family, and my man. I was in a new town, a different world, and that felt strange. I know it was because I was not home, so it was a process for me.

I wanted to learn everything about this sex house. The ins and outs because my goal was to have one of my own. Me and my guy got all of the information. We got the information from Mya who knew the ins and outs but did not know how to work it because she did not know the game.

I had 33 years of street knowledge and 9 years of school knowledge, put that together, that's "Boss" sense. That means that I can go to the end of the world, and come back to where I needed to, I can be in the desert and back to where I need to go and anywhere in the world. I have the knowledge to do what needs to be done.

As time went on, my checks were $18,000 and up, and I got to the point that I was making $30,000 to $40,000 a week. A bad week was $10,000, we built an empire with my family there because we were family.

Five or six months went by, and we all were so close, I thought. But I had been real from day one with my man, with the manager, cook, and housekeeper, and with the owner, with my wife-in-law, the manager.

By wife-in-law, I mean we shared the same man. He was my pimp and hers because I made him that way. That's the way that I taught him. I trained him, so he had learned from the best. He was confident in himself and me.

I believe in God as a little girl so I know I can always call on him no matter where I was at. Yes, I was a sinner for sure, so when I took this work, this is what they had to agree with.

I took control of the house girls, tricks, and housekeepers. What I mean is that I paid them off, whenever I needed something done. I had a dope dealer in town, I had my own house, and when my man stepped off the plane, he no longer had to go to the hotel.

I needed an hour of prayer once a week. I needed to go to my NA meetings because I was in recovery and was coming up on my one-year sobriety day. I take that very seriously, so that was very strange, I felt that I would not figure it out, but life went on.

Chapter 8
Here Comes the Bride

At that time, we were making money and stacking thousands of dollars. Everyone was getting along. The girls were so beautiful. Everything was glamorous. Diamonds from my ears, my hands, on every finger, so there was no turning back if I wanted. We were rolling.

The way I walked, the way I had sex, what I ate, the way I talked, the way I moved, the way I carried myself, it was in a way no other would or could, no one could imitate me or my style. I am a very unique woman.

As time went on, I had a man that I would see on a regular basis. I had lots of men coming and going. I had clientele out of this world. I could not believe that this was going on. I understood what I had, that I was this good. So good, that once a man put it in for three seconds it was over. I never have been very tight from the start and until this day it has not changed.

I knew something was different about me. Everyone wanted to come and see this black, beautiful, sexy woman. Everyone wanted a taste. I would sit down to think about this and still, I could not understand it. At that time, I was working with 10 to 12 women. Very sexy and beautiful women. Blondes, brunettes, browns, redheads, blacks, and all kinds of women.

Women that were so nice. Women with school knowledge but had no street knowledge. You have to have knowledge so that you will know when BS is coming your way, to know when someone is lying or telling the truth.

So, the manager and I took a week off because she was his wife-in-law. We went to Minnesota, and we got a room where we met our men. We had fun and enjoyed ourselves. Yes, we had threesomes, and it was something I would never forget. My man and I had threesomes before, but this was different, something was not right, and I could not put my finger on it.

We always tell each other about everything that is done in the dark will come to the light. So, time went on and on, we went to have breakfast and show her the city. We shopped and had a very good time. As it turns out, everything was almost perfect but only God is perfect. Time went on and we flew back to Elko, Nevada. Back to the sex house and back to work.

So, life was back on track in our house. We had a housekeeper, we had a maid, and we had cooks, we

Chapter 8
Here Comes the Bride

had a swimming pool in the back, we had a privately fenced backyard, and it had a bar, 12 rooms, a bath, and a shower.

It was a small house, but we made the most money on the block. I shut the house down three or four times a week. They had to spend $10,000 or more and then that means no more lineup because I was with him all day and night. He had to spend another $5,000 or more, likely he would spend $10,000 or more because I was good like that.

At the same time, I was into my nine months of sobriety and recovery from crack cocaine. I would not drink anything. Just orange juice, lime, and 7up mixed all together. That's something I thought of so when the guys came in, they wanted to buy me a drink and that was what I had all the time.

They would ask what I drink. I left that up to the bartender to answer that question. I would smile with my beautiful smile, pretty white teeth, big brown eyes, big 38dd, with silk lace satin gown on, my 6-inch heels, smelling so good from head to toe, diamonds on the right side and the left side, four diamonds, and had a diamond ring on everything. I looked like a million dollars. Very beautiful, and breathtaking and I knew it.

CHAPTER 9
Shots Fired, Shots Fired

I LOVED WHAT I did, and my plan was to do this for the rest of my life. But something changed my life forever. I had the Mexican guy that I dated. He would bring his friends in. About 10 of them. He would tell them to date only me, so the house was sewed up for now.

Anyway, on this special day of my life, it was March 13, 1997. I got up in the morning to say my prayers and spend about an hour or so in the shower listening to gospel songs and talking to my grandmom.

I was feeling very strange. I could not put my finger on it to save my life. So, we got a doorbell ring, and the manager buzzed them in. We had to line up. I was picked and I took this Mexican guy back to my room. I had been on dates with him for a while. He came in and gave me the money. I took the money back to the bar, gave it to the manager, and walked back to my room.

I told him he needed to get in the shower, and he said, "Yes". He got in the shower. I went into the bathroom with him and came out. He was still in the shower when I walked out of the shower. I noticed Tabitha coming out of my room. We had a conversation about something. I cannot remember to save my soul.

I said to her, "Why were you in my room". I don't know what she said, so I went back into my room and went back down to the shower to get him. We went to the room and proceeded to my section and was complete. He was very well satisfied.

I put his clothes on and I put his shirt into his pants. I put his boots on and gave him a kiss on his cheek and said goodbye. Then all of a sudden, the doorbell rang, and he and his friends entered with him. He asked to talk to me.

I was at the end of the bar, so he walked toward me and said he wanted to go to the room to talk to me. He really did not say anything. He sat down on my bed and said how he cared for me, and he was acting like something was bothering him.

So, we went back to the bar and had a drink, and he went outside. He came back and rang the doorbell again. At this time, I knew something was truly wrong.

I was standing at the end of the bar again because my room was next to the bar. He came and said he would like to talk to me for the last time. I turned around, my back toward him. All of a sudden, I heard shots go off. 1, 2, 3 times. I knew I was shot. I fell to the floor.

I was hit. So, I called the ambulance and the police or someone. I need help. I pushed myself against the wall, leaned on it, and began to pray. I was so afraid. My eyes were going in the back of my head, my gold robe turned from gold to bloodshot red, and I was on my last breath. I was drifting off. Braden came and said to me, "Are you still with me?" I looked and said, "I'm dying".

I was on my last breath. I knew I was going to die. There was no doubt. But when I said, "I was going to die" I heard a big loud voice and it said, "You are not going to die because I'm not going to let you die."

At that point, I'm trying very hard to look up. I said, "God, with the last breath I have please let me see who shot me." I was going to come back to kill them.

When God gave me strength, I looked up and what I saw was unreal. I saw someone appear in front of me. Had on navy pants, and the shirt was the same color. When I got to the head, he was as big as the sun, white as snow for seconds. I could not look at it anymore. It felt as if heat was coming, then all of a sudden, fear left my body.

The real story behind the shooting
March 3, 1997

The truth and nothing but the truth, so help me God. I started working. I was in Elko, Nevada, and was working at Inez's on 4th Street. Right in front of Mona 1 and Mona 2, across from Sue, and next door to JP. I had been working there for 11 months and the manager at that time was involved with me and my man. That's how I got the job in the first place.

I had agreed for her to have a relationship with us. At that time, I had already discussed it before I left Minneapolis, Minnesota, so everything was fine. Until one day she had friends come over to drink with her. Ladies that worked in the house with her.

They were drinking and talking about everything that came to mind. Whoever they wanted to talk about. This is what my life was about before other things happen in my life.

I was one of the highest paid. I was 5'2. I weighed 130 lbs. I had 38dd and my waistline was 21. My hips were a size 38. I had caramel skin, big brown eyes, a pretty smile, and white teeth. I was well dressed and wore very expensive jewelry. I wore the finest clothes making $10,000 to $50,000 a week. $15,000 is a bad week for me.

In the brothel, the women needed me to talk to their customers because they could not talk the way I could, that's because I had learned the house in and out. It's like you can take a horse to the water but if you don't know how to make him drink, it's nothing.

So, they would have to pay me $1,000 and 2,000 a week, if I made it happen.

It was every woman in the house because they saw how much money I was making. If you cannot beat her, you better pay her, or else you don't make real money. We were a family and we worked together. Me and the manager were wives-in-law and lovers as well. She allowed me to take over the house and to help the girls make money. All was well.

She and I went to Minnesota. She met my kids. We made trips to Reno, Nevada, just to get my hair done. We bought hair for $5,000 from Washington DC. We had it going on. So, we were good.

I had a warrant and she made bail before my plane landed. She took me to the police station, sign my paper, and it was done. Bail had been set.

She bought me a diamond necklace with a custom-made Mercedes enamel on it. Our man would come down after to collect his money and make sure we are emotionally and physically taken care of. We would have a threesome for hours. Life was very good. We had so much money stacked. I was working 7 days a week, 24 hours a day, 365 days a year.

Chapter 9
Shots Fired, Shots Fired

I would stay there 3 months at a time. I had met this man. He had dated me, given me his credit card, and told me to use it forever as long as I got a plane ticket to come to Denver, Colorado to see him. He'd spend $10,000 that day to be with me. I agreed. This was a few months. But I did not know the rules of my license in the state of Nevada.

If I went outside of the house to date someone I met there, I would lose my license in the state of Nevada. So, I took it very seriously. I bought a ring, and I got an airplane ticket because I didn't want to get in trouble. I wanted to do what was right. The manager heard every word he said, and she went to court and spoke on my behalf. It was the truth and nothing but the truth

I did not do any time, but it was on my record. It said unknown on my record, and it was over because I got the plane ticket, and everything went together. I went back to doing my thing and my life was good.

Life went on and on, and she had gotten to the point that she would just talk and talk about our business to her friends. I had the sense to know if she kept talking and the owner found out that she had a pimp, she would be in trouble. I mean in big trouble because he would be thinking she is giving his money to a pimp.

So, it would not have been wise to keep talking about this. It was not good at all. So, she took me to her room, and you will not believe what I saw. A big box with stacks and stacks of money. Hundreds, thousands, and millions of dollars.

She would send the box of money overnight express and put big insurance on it in case it got lost, and that by itself was wrong. They were not paying the IRS because when I said I want to file taxes, the owner said no. I will show you how you can have accounts set up in Switzerland and it would be okay if you made 42,000 in one night.

He came down one day to see who this Mercedes was. He did and it was part of the conversation that he wanted me to sign a five-year contract to work at the sex house, but something happened that changed my life...?

On March 3, 1997, all I remember was getting up that morning. I prayed and listened to some spiritual songs. I called my grandma and talked to her for about an hour. I felt so different that day. It was not like all the other days in my life, but I could not put my hand on it.

I took a shower, put my makeup on, and called my man to see what was happening on the home front. We just bought a home for $270,000 and my sugar daddy had gotten me an 18ft blue and white seaway that sits 15 people. It was 1998. It was new. I had credit cards, I had a GMC, I had a drop-top, and I had about $200,000 of jewelry. So, I had a lot of responsibility.

I had a house in Elko, Nevada. Furniture paid off, paying rent there, and then paid my room off every month. It cost over a thousand dollars a month, tipped my maid, then my cook, then paid for going to the doctor and have everything figure out how to get my money. So, you had to make very good money and then pay a pimp.

This was my choice and that was the lifestyle I live at the age of 14 years. No one by any means made me do anything. If they were not down with that, then I could not deal with that man, under no situation. I moved on.

The only reason why I work there was to find out how they run it in and out. I was going to buy one. My sugar daddy was going to give me $350,000. So that was all good.

Whatever I wanted, I got it, no matter what. I got what I want. I played the game everywhere and was in control in every situation. So, I thought.

When we got a ring on the doorbell, every woman lined up. It was two Mexican guys, and I knew them. They always come when they get their checks every week. I dated him for 11 months and his friend, and he would tell him to date only me. I had it sewed up.

So, I was thinking. We had at that time about 5 to 6 girls working and he picked me. He took off his clothes and I put him in the shower and walked out of the bathroom to check on my room to make sure everything was secure.

That's when I saw one of the girls walk out of my room. I asked what she was doing. She said she is ready to party, and I did not think any more about it. I went back to the shower, went back to the room, and had a very good time for about an hour. I got cleaned up, cleaned him up and we went to the bar happy.

Chapter 9
Shots Fired, Shots Fired

Jesus Save My Life

I thought everything was okay until he asked me to go back to the room with him. I had a very funny feeling about this, this is the same guy I have been dating for almost a year, so I was not worried something was wrong. I wanted to find out what was going on. So, I went to talk to him.

He was acting very, very strange. I asked him, "What is wrong" and he had his head down acting like he was confused. He said to me that he really cared for me. Really, that's what he said. So, I didn't understand what he meant.

We went out of the room and back to the bar. He sat there with his friend. He spoke something in Spanish, but I don't speak that language, so I went back to my room. He left and went outside, him and his friend.

Five minutes later the doorbell rang and thought it was a lineup. It was him and his friend. I stood at the end of the other side of the bar looking. I had on a gold robe with a black lace catsuit, gold heels, and my diamonds. Beautiful as I can be. He came down, he called me back out as I had gone back into my room.

When I called him out, he had his shirt out over his jeans, and he looked so different. When came to me, he said, "I want to talk to you" and I said, "For what, this is the last chance". I turn my back to him and was getting ready to walk through the door and I heard shots go off but did not feel anything. I didn't think it was me, then two more shots went off, and the fourth shot went off and I hit the floor at that time.

He was standing over me. He got hit five times, but I got hit three times. He took off running, he and his friends. Remind you, my man had broken it off with the manager. He said he was done and did not want anything to do with her ever again. He didn't want her money anymore and he never wanted to have sex with her. I knew that in the beginning, but I liked her.

She was very cool until the sex stop with him and her. He said, "If anything happened to Mercedes, I would kill you". So, I said to him, "She is not worth it. She will get hers". We had too much at stake.

At that time, I slid against the wall. My mind told me not to lay down. So, I sat down against the wall. She ran and hollered very loudly and asked me, "If I'm still with them". I said, "I'm dying" and she said, "Hold on they are coming". It was a while, and we were not that far from the police station.

When I said, "I'm dying" I heard a loud voice say, "You're not dying". The living true God himself said it so it caught my attention. It was that powerful. I said when I took those three shots, I started praying to God like never before. Then in the process of waiting and relaxing for the police to get there, I saw a person appear in front. I could not believe this was happening to me, the color was navy blue, and they were the same color.

I was thinking they had come back to finish me off. I prayed and said, "God, please give me strength to see who this was". When I got to the top of his head it was white as the sun. I could look at it for a second because it hurt my eyes.

Fear left my body, and I was not afraid anymore. I had so much faith in God, always believed in God, and was raised up in the church and knew who He was but lost my way along the path. But I always had faith in God. I had a praying grandmother, mom, sister, brother, and people in my family who are saved.

By this time, the police are all over the place and the paramedics are cutting my clothes off. I'm bleeding all over the place. My head is three times bigger than it was. My whole stomach is blown out. They asked me my name and I told them. They asked me for my mom's name and her phone number, and I gave it to them.

I got strength all of a sudden and at that point, he breathed life back into my body until I was so overtaken. I could not tell you in a million years what God had done for me. I was sweating. It was so unspeakable and unchangeable. My life was never the same.

I felt very different at that moment. My eyes left this man, I said, "It was the son of God himself" At that time, the police and ambulance were there and the whole place was surrounded by people.

They were asking what I did to deserve this. The police said, "It doesn't matter what she did, she didn't deserve this". They said some money was missing. They searched my room from top and bottom and came up with nothing. So, they were very upset that I had been shot and was on my deathbed. I had been hit three times.

I was in the ambulance and the person that appeared to me, his face turned human. I watched him the whole time I was in there.

They put in an IV, oxygen, and a whole lot of things to try to keep me alive. They said, "Send the helicopter back, that I would not make it because my liver, my kidneys, my spleen, my colon, and one of my lungs was hit." I was torn all to pieces.

They rush me to the hospital and into the emergency room. I was on my way to the operating room when they decided what they were going to do about me. One doctor said, "We can give her a bag" and the other doctor said, "Her insides are very good" so we will put her pieces back together".

As I was going to surgery, the guy that shot me, came through the door with the police and he identified me going to surgery. So, I told the police he had shot me. I knew he was on drugs, and they wanted him to be tested.

So, God is good. I went to surgery for six hours and came out of surgery. Those were the worst days of my life. I was hooked up to every kind of machine they had in there. There was something big running into my heart. I was on a breathing machine, tubes going down my throat, and in my nose. It was a mess.

I could not talk, walk, or breathe on my own. I was dying. They did not expect me to live. So, I fought for my life with prayer, faith, and hope. I know the living and true God we serve he is alive, active, and well. Jesus sits at the right hand of his Father. The Holy Spirit is the helper, so I had all the help I needed.

I had God all by himself, so to God be the glory. I fought in my spirit and prayed. As time went on, days and days went by, I fought for my life because all the material things I had did not matter.

The Shooter

Let's go back to the person that shot me. He was so upset about what he had done to me. He tried to get away. He ran into the back of this lady and took off. The police saw everything that happened and were now on a high-speed chase.

The police ran him off the road. When they stopped him, he noticed something was wrong for real. So, he said he was going to take him back.

Chapter 9
Shots Fired, Shots Fired

He was okay at the same time. He took the gun from his friend. They caught him when he gave it to him. So, he was going to check the gun out. When they bought him to the hospital, as they were bringing him in, I was passing by while he was walking through, and I identified him from my bed as I was going to surgery. They took him into custody right then and there. That's how good God is.

Now, I'm fighting for my life. They said my kidney, liver, colon, spleen, and both lungs were damaged. The bullet was a half inch from my spine. I was in surgery for 6 hours. When I got out of surgery, the first person I saw was my mom. She was hurting. She had tears in her eyes. Then I knew for the first time in my life that she really loved me.

I was hooked up to every machine you could think of. It was a mess. A rubber tube was running down into my heart, my head was three times the size of a watermelon. My eyes closed, but I could open them a little. Tubes were running into my mouth. They had me on a breathing machine. I was not breathing on my own. They worked and worked on me, and I went into a coma for 16 days.

I did not know what was going to happen but what I did know, when I got that third shot, I heard a voice say, "You are not going to die because I'm not going to let you die." I know without a shadow of a doubt it was God. He came off his throne because I was a woman of faith. No matter what I was doing, I knew I had been a sinner for a very long time. But all I could think about was God. I believed that he could heal me without a doubt.

I had always believed in God but for some reason, I was not living right. My family was right, most of them and not all of them. We all at one point do things that are not right.

Then, my boyfriend showed up, my mother did not like him. Why? I never knew. But I was in the fight of my life. I prayed like I never prayed before. My God, that was one of the saddest days of my life.

The doctor came in. People and nurses were everywhere. A lot was going on. After seventeen days, the doctor said they had done all they could do.

They took me off the machines. They unhooked the breathing machine. They were all so sad and said they give me about six hours to live. I feel like I had been run over by a semi-truck. My life had taken the turn for the worse. But I knew what the Lord had spoken to me.

I have faith that you would not believe. That was all I had. No one but God. When your body gets cold, your heart stopped, your tongue is at the top of your throat, your body is still, then your spirit goes out of your body. It is only you and God.

Your mom, dad, sister or brother, or grandparents cannot help you. But God has the strength and the "power" to bring you through. This is the way I always have felt. But this was the first time, I ever thought like this.

I held on to everything I had and that was God the living God, the true and living God, and Jesus, the son of God and Holy Spirit is the help. It is the action. It is the one to get God's job done. I kept on holding on to God's unchanging hand because he had me in the palm of his hand.

They took it all off and I was in a lot of pain. I was in so much pain. I was fighting for my life. I asked my mom to go and get my clothes from the house. I ask her to go and get my pajamas, house shoes, and robe.

Then go to the bank and get everything that belongs to me.

I asked her to go home and go back to work. I told her I would be home soon. I love her very much. My man was also there at my bedside.

When my mom returned with my things, no one had seen me move. My nurse was the sheriff's daughter. She gave me some phone numbers of lawyers if I lived. I had a very high temperature. That night she gave me an ice bath and my temperature went down. They said they did not have to do surgery on me. That was a blessing.

So, getting back. I was getting ready to put on my pajamas. I asked everyone to leave the room so I can get dressed. When I looked at my body, I wanted to fall out. I had 72 stitches, bullet holes in my back, and scars everywhere. I had never had scars or stretch marks or anything on my stomach. Yes, I had tattoos, but you couldn't see them. I kept them covered, but to wake up to a nightmare like this, it seemed my life was over. So, I thought it was.

This was the worst thing that could ever happen to me. But my grandma always said you reap what you sow. That is very true. If you sow a bad seed, then a bad seed is coming. If you sow a good seed, then a good seed is coming. So, that is very true.

So, I continued to fight for my life. When my mom brought my pajamas, I asked everyone to leave. But before they left, I asked for the believers to come and pray with me and God moved like the wind, stirring up things.

Then I took a shower, put on my pajamas, and went outside in the hallway. Everyone was outside looking at me.

I began taking baby steps, then a little walk from one end to the other. As I walked, I could picture God carrying me. I knew he was with me. He has always been with me. He was there even when I didn't know it.

So, I stayed at the hospital for a little while longer. Then I had to leave but I could not get on a plane and fly home. I was too fragile. So, Miss Madeline let me stay over her house for a few months until I had enough strength to fly.

After about four months, they set it up with the airport with Minnesota airlines to have a wheelchair ready when I got off the plane. When I arrived, my mom was there to take me home.

After I got home, I did not talk a lot. I felt so ashamed about everything that I was doing. I did a lot of things, but now what was I going to do with my life? I should not have been in the brothels.

So, before I left Nevada, I went to court a few times about the guy that shot me. He got 10 years in prison. He had to do 95% of his time, but in 5 years, I said let him free because I felt in my heart it was more to the story than what he was saying. I will get to the root of this, and all the world will see it.

A lot was going on in my case. I had a civil case pending and one day I had to go to settle out of court. But I was not feeling like anything that day. So, I did not show up.

The lawyer on his side got the judge to throw the case out saying it cannot be tried in the state of Nevada. So, I'm going to the Supreme Court of Nevada. If that does not work, I'm going to the Supreme Court in Washington DC, and let God move on my behalf.

Chapter 9
Shots Fired, Shots Fired

Trying to Make it Work

Things got really bad with me and my man. I lost the desire to be with him and to be the owner of a brothel. My dream was shot forever. I was very, very, very angry at God and myself. I had hate in my heart.

I hated myself. I hated my man because I blamed him. This was his fault. However, when I look at the situation, it was all my fault. I made the decision to do the things I had done. It was my fault but at that time I could not see it, and I couldn't see it for a very long time.

But God. What would we do without God? How could I have made it this far if it was not for God? I have to praise him. I have to glorify him at all times.

I went to rehabilitation to learn how to walk, talk, and get my life back together. That was a hot mess. I had to hold onto God's unchanging hand as he makes and breaks me. I did not know what at that time. But God makes no mistakes. He is in control.

He can do whatever he wants. He is God alone and I'm so proud and glad that he is truth, pure, the Almighty. His ways are not like the ways of people. He is not a liar. He is perfect and I love him.

I make it up in my mind to be a servant. Serving God like I know he is not a person, but he is real. So real, I can't see him, but I know he is there. I can feel his presence. I will be very happy to see all three in one. That is the trinity. Father, Son, and Holy Ghost.

So, time went on and I had made up my mind when I got where I was going to leave Levi. Anyway, he turned and became very mean to me because I spent a night out. I had lost my mom to cancer and stayed over Samuel's house that night. He was comforting me and cooked me breakfast in bed. That was it. But my man thought I had an affair. He was wrong.

From the start, I promised him that I would only have him. He must have forgotten I knew that he was sleeping with someone else. Whomever it was they were dirty because every time I went to the doctor, I would have an infection. I knew he was doing it, but he would not tell me the truth about what he was doing.

I was always at work. But one day I came home to surprise him and there was a woman in my house. I knew who she was, He had told me that he wanted to have sex with her. He said he was going to wait on me. He lied about that too.

I knew what was going on, but I let it slide. So, I no longer wanted to be with him. When he returned home that morning when I got home from work, he was there waiting for me. He hit me when I stepped in the front door.

My friend was there. She was there for my mom's funeral, so she stayed at my house. He started beating me until blood was coming out. He grabbed me by my shirt and pull me out of the house with his 9 mm. He said he was going to kill me. If he could not have me no one else would.

Then he put me in the truck that I bought for him. He also had the gun that I brought for him. So, there we are going somewhere I had never been or seen. I heard a voice tell me "Jump out". So, I let the window down to jump. God helped me and I ran inside the store. I did not have a shirt on. He had taken it off me.

I called my sister, and she called him. At that point, he was not my man. So, I let my sister use his car to come and get me. She did and I went to her house for a few days. Then I went back, and things were not cool.

He did not put his hands on me. But I was still not going to be with him anyway because of what he had done and had been doing. I was not going to argue about it. I was just going to get out.

CHAPTER 10
Watch God Move

THE SPIRIT STARTED to speak to me about so many things at different times, different prophets, prophetesses, bishops, pastors, and evangelists. It was a revelation. All these people of God were telling me the truth. So, I began to pray and pray unto God. Give me power and authority because the word will not come back void.

If he said he was going to do something, it can be 30 years later, he is the same God. Moses, John, and Peter prayed, and Abraham, Isaac, and Jacob believed in the same living and true God. Today, the Holy Spirit has been sent to us because Jesus has already conquered hell and death when he went to the cross.

My life began to change quickly because God said I did not know who I was in Christ or what was my purpose, but God showed me through the prophet. One day, I was at church praising and worshiping the Lord and he had robed me.

On the back of my robe, it was white trim with gold and God allow my sister to see this. He allowed her to tell me I was anointed and that's when I knew I was called by God, chosen by God, and anointed by God before the foundation of the world. Before I was born, God had a plan for my life.

But I was even more afraid because I had sinned more than anyone who ever walked this earth. I was confused but there were two things I knew to do. Number one, pray. Number two, have faith.

If I prayed about it, God was going to come down and do it no matter what it was. If I was in the valley, he was coming. If I was in a fiery furnace, he was coming. If I was on my deathbed, he was coming. If I was in prison, he was coming. If I was sick, he was coming. If I died and he wanted me to live, then I will.

Now it was very clear to me who He is. I recognize this man we call the Almighty. He is the beginning and the end. He is the first and the last. He is my mother, father, brother, sister, aunt, uncle, and grandma, He is my husband and is my best friend. People will always fail you, but God, Son, and Holy Ghost will never leave you, nor forsake you.

Life started taking a turn for the good. I was walking and talking and thinking so differently. I was so in awe, and I could not explain it if I wanted but I can see it in the spiritual realm. God telling Satan, "I commanded you to take your hands off her, you had her for 35 years and I allowed you to do this to her, but you will not kill her. I'm taking her back for my glory. Watch what she is going to do. She will be the woman that I made her to be."

She will glorify me, and she will go to the nations, she was a general in the world and now she will be a general for me. She will move in power. I have given her authority on this earth, and she will walk in deliverance, and you cannot have her anymore. You watch, no more."

I began to walk with power. O' my, I began to prophesy to the people. God said, "You are a prophet because I made you one and you will bring people out of places no one else ever has. You are the ram in the bush that I have cleansed, purified, and washed. I broke you, shaped you, and put what I want in you, and what I want out of you, Maudell.

I'm your God. I can do whatever I want. Know that you did not do anything to get this because I made a promise to you long ago that if you said, "Yes". I know everything you will do because I'm God. I laid this foundation. I'm the foundation."

To change my life God sent to me his prophet to prophesy to me, to tell me things that will come. A prophecy is something that is coming to pass because the Holy Spirit said it.

You see the Holy Spirit is the action of God. He is my teacher and my trainer, and he gets God's job done through people. He doesn't make mistakes. He does what God says and only what he says.

This is the way I put it. He is God's brain. God is the creator, Jesus is the son of the living true God, and the Holy Spirit is the helper. So, I'm so glad that Jesus came and died for our sins, but I was sad just to know that's why he came.

I don't deserve anything from God. It is God that I sinned against, and I ask Him for forgiveness. I repented of all my sins, seen and unseen, known and unknown. God remembers everything, even if I don't, that is a good and perfect God who is living without fault.

My Season of Deliverance

I got my first prophecy in Cone Rapids at the Community Center. I had just gotten back from Pahrump, Nevada. That Saturday night I flew in and went to my sister's house. The next day was Sunday and my sister asked me if I wanted to go to church. I said, "I don't have anything to wear to church." Not that I didn't have clothes, just not church clothes.

She said she has something for me to wear. I said, "Okay" and we went to church. This would happen every time I went home. For some reason, I wanted to go but I just could not put my hand on it, but I knew in my heart and soul it was something going on with me and God.

So, we went to church. We were singing, praising, worshiping, and listening to the word of God and he started to prophesy. He called me up there, I would never forget it, and he said to me, "Daughter, God said, "He loves you so much and if you would say yes, He would move heaven and earth for you."

Now that right there took me to a different call. I didn't know what was going on, but I knew something was different. Right then and there, I began to cry and hurt. I was so sad because I was so lost and did not know what to do or how to do it.

My life went on and on and even when I was working in brothels, it was under serious conditions for me to pray for one hour and for me to spend time working on sobriety time by myself. I was in recovery, but I knew God since the age of five, okay.

My grandmother would always be talking to someone that I could not see. I asked my grandmother to whom she was talking. She said, "God" and began to tell me about who Jesus was and why He went to the cross for our sins.

Chapter 10
Watch God Move

So, I knew God and I went to church every Sunday. We went to choir practice once a week, but she was in the church at least three times a week.

As I went on in life, even in my days of smoking crack cocaine, I would talk to God all the time asking him to help me and asking him how I ended up in this mess. I questioned God all the time because I did not understand how my life was going to go. I figured that I would die at the age of 17.

Time went on and on until I got into recovery, and God delivered me from crack cocaine. From 13 years of getting high. God delivered me from a lesbian spirit. I was with a woman for 15 years of my life. My life was a mess, upside down, uncontrollable, out of control, and confusing and I was about to lose my mind.

As time when on, God continued to change my life. The bad behavior started to change. I started to walk a little differently. In 2005, God changed my life like never before. From the start, I had been through so much in my lifetime, until I just made it up in my mind, that I was going to say "Yes" to this God everyone is talking about.

Their lives had been changed because of Jesus Christ. Now, at that time, I had more knowledge than I ever had before. I was at my sister's church and her pastor spoke to me and said, "God said that He is giving you a new wardrobe. Get ready to have it made." When he said, "Robe" I knew what he was saying but did not really understand.

I would do it and I did, and the lady started making them. She only wanted money. So, God pointed me to another woman. Not just anyone, but a real woman of God. She began to explain about making garments and how sacred it was to have someone to make your robe.

They should pray over the garment, and they should be holy and anointed. She is like a mother to me to this day. She is still making my garments. I love Ms. Susannah so much. She has wisdom and knowledge.

A Miracle in the Middle of a Mess
Understand what I'm saying, we can do all things, the worldly things, and when you get in any situation, it's only you and God. He is the only one who can

bring you out. You will face that one day. All of us must.

It's life and everyone has to die because Jesus died for our sins. He did not have any sin in him. He was without a spot or blemish. He came not to condemn the world but to save it. So, be a believer, not walking and doing things that are not of God.

I was out of the will of God and that allowed the devil to eat me alive. I fought for my life in the hospital for 16 to 19 days. I took a turn for the worst. My fever went up and they wanted to do surgery. My nurse was the sheriff's daughter.

She was a very good nurse. She is the one that gave me the lawyer's number and said to me, "If you live you would be taken care of for the rest of your life. This should not have happened to you."

So, they wanted to do another surgery on me. My nurse knew that, so she gave me an ice bath to bring my temperature down. It stayed down. I thank God for her. I didn't have to have surgery.

I took a turn for the worse again. I had fluid in my lungs, and they had to get it out so I could breathe. They gave me a spinal tap. They put two big, long needles in my back. I could not move, or I would have been paralyzed for the rest of my life.

They did it, and it was okay, but I was still in pain. I mean my whole body was in pain. So, I was fighting in the natural and I was standing in faith. The living true God had it all worked out in the spirit. That's why I had to stand on the word of God. Without faith it isn't possible to please God (Hebrews 11:6). That was all I knew at the time.

Left to Die

Days went by and finally, the doctor said that they have done all they can do. I would not live. They gave me 6 hours to live. That was the worst thing I had heard. They unplugged me from every machine I was hooked up to. The only thing they left was my IV and then they left me to die.

The first person that I saw was my mom. She was there from the start. Her and my man. He was now my ex-man. But God is good.

Time went on and on and on. I told my mom to go and get my clothes and everything I owned. I will be coming home, I promise. I told her that because I had only faith in God. Not in myself. So, I asked my mom to go to buy me some pajamas, house shoes, and a robe for me to wear. She did. Bless her heart. She bought them back for me to shower and put them on.

I asked everyone to leave my room and I got up. I remind you, the doctor said I would die and that I would never walk or talk again, and if I lived, I would be paralyzed for the rest of my life. They left the room, and I got in the shower, but my mom stayed with me the whole time. I put on my pajamas, my robe, and house shoes and she opened the door open.

Everyone on the floor was looking and some were crying because they could not believe what they were seeing because I was already counted out. For someone to hear that you got shot, and you just died, I was already counted out. But God said no! He bought me through, and I am very grateful that we serve a God like that.

Time went on, I sent my mom back to Minnesota where I was from so, she can go back to work. God already had everything set up. Even though I did not know His plan for my life.

Mom left and I was taken to another place. To a good person's house, her name was Ms. Natalie. She worked in the house I got shot in, so I stayed there until I was able to get on the plane. My body was very fragile, the doctor said I could not make it to the airport right now.

So, later when I got better, when I got stronger and stronger, the owner of the house was on the way to come see me. He was bringing me an offer.

My lawyer was also on the way to see me and told me not to talk to them and that he would take care of everything, that I need to be taken care of. So, I said, "Yes". My lawyer came and I signed a paper about my case, and they talked with me, but they had to do most of the talking because I was in a very big mess. I was in pain. All I could do was just pray and pray.

My voice sounded like a man's. It was so heavy. I had 72 stitches in my stomach. I had scars under my left arm where they had to run rubber tubes. There were bullet holes all over my back.

I was so ashamed of myself. I was hurt. I had hate in my heart. Bitterness had set in, and I hated Mexicans because the person that shot me was Mexican. I wanted to kill him and his whole family. I was a hot mess and did not know how to deal with it. I was mad at God for allowing this to happen to me.

He did not by no means. He did not do this to me, He just allowed it, it was through my bad choices, sin, and being disobedient on the road of destruction. There was warning after warning, then destruction set in. But God was there with me all the way. He had me in the palm of his hand and no demon or Satan could pluck me out of his hands.

This is why I was going to Andrew to court. He flew down to see me, to talk about me signing a contract with him for 5 years and to help me to invest my money in stocks and to open an account in Switzerland. I made him all these millions, but when I got shot, he was not there. He sent flowers like I was going to die. They were so big you could have put them on my casket.

So, I went home to my house, where my man and I stayed. Yes, we stayed together. We were very close. Yes, I was in love with him and his son. That was our son and I still love our son and wish him and his father well.

I was upset for no reason. When I look at it today, he is the only one that was in the game with me that did what he said he was going to do. So, we were going to get married, but I ended up leaving him. Our sex was not the same. I was ashamed to take off my clothes because of my scars. I was ashamed and depressed, and my emotions were all over the place.

I knew in my heart he was sleeping with other women behind my back. I kept catching different infections that were sexually related. He would always lie about it. He should have kept it 100%. A lot of people can't say that because they cannot keep it 100%. They are not. I know without a doubt, that I used safe sex with every trick. My man was the only one I had sex with without condoms. I love him so much, but I knew in my heart he had to go.

CHAPTER 11
Open for Business

MY BABY SISTER was involved with this guy, and he wanted me to meet his friend, but I was always traveling all over the world. Flying here and there. Every time he was in town, I was not. Every time I was in town, he was not. But one day, we did meet.

We sat and talked and talked. The very first thing that came to my mind was, "Was this very nice-looking man single?" I felt something was wrong with this picture. I was right.

Years and years later, my man that I was with when I got shot, his name is TJ. After the shooting, my mom took a turn for the worse. Her life was never the same after I got shot. She went down after that, and she died on September 25, 1998, the same time I got married to my sugar daddy. My life was so messed up from what it was before I got shot.

I ended up leaving TJ and my life took the turn for the worse. I lost my house because I could no longer afford my mortgage, boat payment, or anything. My bills were around $10,000 or more a month with everything I had. This is what I recall.

The day came for them to bring me an offer. I was still in treatment to learn how, to walk, to hold my head up, and to just learn who I was again. They wanted me to fly to Nevada for that, but I was not feeling well.

I said, "I wasn't going to be able to come now. What would be more important? For me to be there?" That was more important to me than life itself at this time. So, my lawyer called me, and I said, "I have a warrant".

So, they went to court to ask the judge to throw it out, so it cannot be tried in the state of Nevada. I think the judge and my lawyer were paid off. They gave me

Chapter 11
Open for Business

$9,000 to take my case and now they just walked away from a high-profile case that was worth 13 million dollars. I was suing for 10 million myself. My mom was suing for 3 million. So, I went on believing that it was nothing that I could do about it.

I called the Supreme Court in 2002 to ask them about my case. They said it was dismissed without prejudice. I asked what that means. It means it can be tried again. I called and left messages with some lawyers and no one would take it. I know why because of who I'm suing. Because he has money and lots of it and money is power in this world.

I cannot go on in life knowing that I had been done wrong. Justice has not been served. There are people involved in my shooting who believe that they have gotten away. They think that justice will not be served.

Yes, I have a criminal background dating back to 1989. But what does that have to do with what happened to me? I didn't do anything to deserve this.

The police knew what was on my record when they gave me licenses. I had my license with the state of Nevada since 1995. Everything was good. I was making everyone money. It was good. Now that I have been shot and almost died in a brothel, everyone in the town wants me to go away.

But that is not going to happen. If something was to happen to me, this would be the only reason why.

I gave my life to Christ in 2005. I said, "Yes" 100%, and before I try to make money in Pahrump Cherry Patch and Chick Ranch, because they said in Elko, Nevada, that I would never work in that town again.

I'm the one that got shot, so what is wrong with this picture? I would never give up because I'm a very determined person. I will go public, to the news, and everywhere. I will be heard, and justice will be done. All I ask is to reopen my case in the Supreme Court in Washington DC so I can get a fair trial. It was a civil case, and the truth shall come out.

I have allowed God to change my life completely. I have given up prostitution. I have gotten those kinds of men out of my life. I don't run with anyone if they're not moving for God or doing the right thing. I'm a mother, a grandmother, a sister, and a daughter, and most of all, I'm a woman of God.

Chapter 11
Open for Business

He has chosen me to preach the word, and nothing can come between that. I am waiting for my man of God, which will be my husband. I will love him and do right by my God first, then my husband, then my family, my spiritual family, and then my natural family whom I love.

I have great compassion for people today. I did not have that at one point in my life. I have been clean from crack cocaine for more than 15 years and have been doing the will of God since 2005, so all I ask is for justice to be done. Let the people pay for what they have done.

There is one person who has been trying to tell the truth about what happened. God will have his way. The Sheriff at that time said they knew who had something to do with my shooting. Even if they did, I just want the truth to come out.

Therefore, I cannot have closure until the matter is done. It will not go away. It will make headlines everywhere until justice is served. Then my life will be complete.

I can go on in life. I would like to do a biography on my shooting and a book. May God have his way, in Jesus name.

Open for Business

Mercedes Place. Mercedes Braids and Beauty Supply. Mercedes Hair Beauty Supply. I had a store on 2124 West Broadway, which today is a cellular store owned by a good friend of mine.

My grand opening was going to be on October 5, 1999, but I went to prison on August 4, 1999. I trusted my boyfriend to take care of everything in life instead of depending on God who is solid, and I know is a rock and cannot be moved.

I built my life on sand that will go down. I was a fool without brains. That was the first store. The second store was located at 1816 ½ Central NE. There was a drug house upstairs over my store. God showed me that.

I had a third store. God gave me a vision about this store, and He blessed me to come across the person to help me. He's spent a lot of money in that store. For that reason alone, I'm grateful.

Chapter 11
Open for Business

I thank him for all he has done for me. The Mercedes Braids and Beauty Supply was one of the most beautiful stores I ever had. I allowed myself to get into a situation that I did not need to be in. Being hardheaded, I did it anyway and I paid for it.

I close my store down on my own without asking God and it cost me everything. I had worked so hard to get this store open. It took God and me, 33 days to finish

Mercedes Braids

When you walk in there were green marble floors and when you go up there were birchwood floors. I had a big living area with a 42-inch flat-screen TV. I had a salon on one side. It had a black countertop and beauty chairs. Black track light over the whole store. I had a glass showcase made of birchwood and a reception desk made of the same wood.

I had a receptionist answering the phone and greeting people on the other side. I had hair, wigs, shoes, jeans, Ed Hardy, eyelashes, supplies, and sunglasses. There were cameras set up everywhere. A glass cut out, where I can see you, but you cannot see me.

Back in my office, was everything a woman can have. My bathroom was different colors every week and going back to the dressing room, there was a 52-inch flat-screen TV. You walked on green marble floors all the way to the dressing room office.

There was a secret code and only the employees knew it. Outside of my office was a wash and dry, the one that runs $2,220 per set and was registered only for the people that worked in the store. Everything in the store was new from the top to the bottom. Well over $150,000 in a store which is not that much to me. I love to have the best.

CHAPTER 12
Law Enforcers, Lawyers, and More

TO THE POLICE, US Marshals, FBI, and secret service, first and foremost I want to say, "Hello". Having been a part of some of your lives, I know you will be surprised by how my life has changed. You know who I am, Miss Maudell Hardison.

I had many affairs with the police. One office would take other people's dope and mine, put only me in the cop car, and take me far away. He would give me my dope back and make love to me.

This went on until I left the drug scene. Then I went a little higher to the FBI. One thing I knew, is the good ones keep their word if you are loyal. No, I'm not a snitch. We got things done. If you were on my side, you were good. I did not set anyone up. This is very personal, and this still exists.

My guard at my conferences will be real security because of the lifestyle I have lived. I'm scared but very wise. But God has changed my life, so they will support me in this ministry as they are good people. The bad ones, I pray that they are gone.

For all my judges, lawyers, and prosecutors. Yes, them. They were all tricks and done very well by me. See, I had men in very high places. I even had doctors at the Clinic, they know who they are. But I would never call them out for no amount of money or fame. I'm still a very loyal, trustworthy, and honest person.

This was my life, but God changed my life and my way of thinking. I'm not of the world anymore. I work for God, the true and living God, Jesus the son of the living God. The Holy Spirit is my teacher and trainer. He is the action of God. I say He is God's brains.

Chapter 12
Law Enforcers, Lawyers, and More

He gives me commandments to live by and obey. He has authority over me. You never see me take my brother or my sister to court because God is the judge, amen.

Prison life in Shakopee
Minnesota to Pahrump Nevada

Well, I was on paper for 8 months and I needed to make more money. I knew the only way I could do this quickly was to go to Nevada where prostitution was legal. The problem was I was on paper in Minnesota. I knew that I was taking a very big chance with what I was about to do because you have to go to the police to get a prostitution license.

I discussed it with him for me to go to Nevada. Then, I prepared to go there. When I flew into Las Vegas, my limousine driver was there. Braden took me to the doctor to get checked out. It was good. I then went to the police station and got my license. He then took me to the strip until I was cleared to work. Then my limousine driver came to the strip to get me to go to work.

When I got to the house, I took a shower, put on my makeup, and got dressed to get on the floor. At

Cherry Patch, there is the number one and the number two house. You have to be between 110 to 145 pounds for the number one house, and between 150 to 300 pounds for the number two house.

Some men like big girls too. I got dressed and was ready to make money. I took care of my business.

I worked at the number two house. Not because I was too fat for the number one house, but because they had too many girls in the house, so they made room for me. I work for 9 days, and my boss came to me, and he said, "Why didn't you tell me that you were on paper in Minnesota?"

So, he said they said I have 5 days to get home. So, I went and got ready to leave so that I could fly back to Minnesota. He cashed me out.

I left there, returned home, and went to see my probation officer. He set a court date. I was just getting ready to open up my store. My grand opening date was October 5, 1999. I went to court. I took my briefcase with all my papers where I had worked.

I had on over $100,000 worth of jewelry. I had $8,000 in cash and drove a 430 Lexus. I had a $270,000 house and a drop-top convertible, a GMC truck, and an 18 ft sea boat, and had spent about $50,000 in the store. We had 5 lbs. of grass, and the house was laid out from top to bottom.

I went to court on August 4, 1999. They took me to prison. It was my first time going. When I got there, I went to RO for a week. I met this woman named Brook. She was my RO teacher. She taught me the rules and regulations of the prison. She kept spending time with me, so I knew something was up.

So, we were kicking it with each other. She was about money and what they do in the prison to get money and the canteen, that was what they were about. It did not take all that. Just be real with people. I was her man.

I let it be known when I leave this prison, I'm going to my man. Everyone knew it. So, time went by, and Brook and I got together. I was still bi-sexual, so I was okay with it. I bought canteen for us, and we were in the same unit, so it worked out very well. We were in Roosevelt, which was intake for new women.

So, life went on and my man came to visit me and send me letters every other day. I had thousands and thousands on my books, so we could shop like that. It was very good. My sugar daddy put money on my books every week. Whatever I spent was getting put back on my book. So, we were good.

I treated her fair, like everyone else. I would speak to people everywhere and I minded my own business. I saw things but I didn't say anything. Their problems were their problems, only I was like everyone else, and I was still in the world, so I kept my things like ice cream, cheese, and chicken and what else we had.

One day, they called me to the office and asked me if I gave anyone permission to go into my things. I said, "No" because I did not think for one minute that they were telling me about her because I bought her whatever she wanted. I even put money on the books. $500. She could hold her own. She was just greedy. At that time, I could not see it.

So, they took her to the hole. I was very upset about it and with her because if she needed something she should have asked me. I would have given it to her.

So, life went on and I got with someone else. Her name was Terry. She was a bigger mess. So, all they wanted to do is mess over people and they didn't care how each other felt.

Chapter 12
Law Enforcers, Lawyers, and More

So, time went on. I worked in the kitchen and went to school every day. I had classes, went to church, had visits, and went to anger management classes and o victim impact classes. I went to Loss and Grief classes. It was very good for me.

When she got out of the hole, I had moved on with someone else. I was a hot mess too, but I was a very good person, a very good-hearted person. Time went on and I sent her money on her book and moved on.

I went to work release at 444 Lyn Hurst Street, St. Paul, Minnesota. My sugar daddy came up and bought $100 of crab legs for me and the girls and went shopping to buy a towel, bed comforter, radio, sheets, and CD player, and I got my nails done.

I worked at the factory, had visits, and I felt good about myself. I was good. I had lots of jewelry and nice clothes. I had to do 90 days and when it came close for me to get out, I had 3 days left, they called me into the office and arrested me.

I bonded out on a $50,000 bail bond. My man Marcus came to get me in 2 hours, so it was good. They let me go home and it was straight. I went to meet my new parole officer and that was good. He and

I got along with each other. I stayed on paper for 90 days until I expired off of it.

Here We Go Again

When my man and I, broke up, I went straight to another sugar daddy. We went out and it was a long time before we were intimate. He was a very clean man. He was very unique, very well-dressed, and a very smooth talker.

We went out because I was still hurt about what me and my man went through. We talked to get to know each other. He said he did you wrong and I would never do you that way or hit you. I'm a lover, not a fighter.

I was lost. I was so messed up in my head and confused. I was not ready for another relationship and knew that I was in my flesh. I was big-time double-minded, so twisted in every way. You would have thought I would have had some space between the two relationships. I did not.

I kept on going and going like a Duracell battery. I kept on going and going. I was playing papers, and lots of traveling, all over the world and in every state. So, I was traveling and trying to pick up the pieces of my life.

After I got out of prison, he had me and he would visit me, and send cards that smelled good, so I was very happy. When he came, he was always looking so good and dark sexy chocolate. I say he was the same color as a Snickers. He was my snicker bar.

My feelings were getting so involved. We went out, we had dinner, and we spent a lot of time together. At that time, I was a dancer, prostitute, a paper chaser. I played many parts in my life. I was a mother, and sister, I had a man, and I was a daughter, so I had many paths, but I should have been on one path.

When I was in prison in 1999, all the women and I were all together. I went to RO and I met Lilly. She taught me the rules and regulations of the prison. We stayed in RO for two weeks, so that I and the other women could know the rules of the prison.

As time went on, I did not need him to give me money because I had thousands on my books. Thank God for that. He came to see me every week and wrote me every day. I was all right with that. One day when he came to see me, he said he was not a pimp. He was a player for sure.

He said he met this woman, and she is down with us, but she kept saying to me, this girl keeps on saying she has a friend named Mercedes and he said I got a woman named Mercedes. She is my number one. Because she is qualified to me be my number one, she is running everything down here.

Time went on and I got out of prison. I went to work release and he came to see me as soon as he could. I put him as my husband on my list. Remember, I said earlier in my writing that I was married to a sugar daddy. He lived in Iowa, so that's the way things were.

He came to see me. He bought this woman over to see if she knew me. When I came to the door he was standing there, and she was too. I could not believe it was her. I was glad and sad, my emotions started running away from me, but I had to keep them under control. I knew and understood the game. I had been living in the game for a very long time, so I had to accept this for what it was.

I got a job working at the factory and my man would bring me food for lunch and have lunch with me. As time went on, he told me he had Netty. He had knocked up a prostitute. I knew it was going to be some mess in the game. That's how I felt when he said she was a nurse. I was a call girl, traveling, and making money all over the state. Then he came and told me about this.

Now a real pimp would have said I knocked a prostitute, end of the story. That's when I realized he was not a pimp, but a player. My friend was a tramp. For sure, I did have a problem with it because we had been friends for years. I thought everything was good with me being his number one. Being number two I thought we would big up again like me and My man. I thought it would have done everything for him or with him.

As time went on, I really trusted him with my life. He had not given me a reason to distrust him yet. Anyway, one day I got off work and I had three days left in work release. They told me to come into the office. When I did, they told me that I had a warrant for my arrest.

I signed all my papers over to one of my close sugar daddies. My property and my jewelry. I asked this lady

I knew to call him to tell him that I had been arrested and taken to Ramsey County. He set bond on a $50,000 bail and came to get his baby. You know by that he must care at this point. I did not think he loved me.

He came to get me with her, and they picked me up and drove my truck. She was driving. He is quick to trust women. So, I thought about that. But that was just the way he was. He loved everyone. He would not mistreat anyone. But it was okay.

But I guess you cannot teach an old dog new tricks. I understood to the depth of my soul what it was. So, I rolled with it and now he left me a note to meet him at the bail bond not that far away. So, I did. When I got there, he was not there. So, I waited for him.

They pulled up in my truck. We hugged each other. He got in the back, and I drove. She was in the front with me.

Before I would talk to her on phone and would tell her how to have oral sex with him because there was no doubt, that I was one of the best. He said I did this thing for a living. I was not just good, I mastered sex and I knew it. I could turn it on and off.

Chapter 12
Law Enforcers, Lawyers, and More

So, on the phone, she knew what it was, and he wanted me to make sure she knew this was the real deal. He may not have been a pimp, but he had me. One of the best. He was my baby, right or wrong. It was okay when I was locked up.

He was the best I had in bed to be perfectly honest. I would give him a Ph.D. in sex. He was the best. The two of us together were like an earthquake. It's just right for me and him. So, it was okay when she was alone with him. But when mom came home, there was a problem. The problem is she was not a real slut. Never was.

He was the kind of person you can say this is what it is, but I need this for this, and he would say, okay baby. That was cool with me because I knew what kind of person he was. We were at the northland for a week in a two-bedroom Jacuzzi suite and $120,000, and all he said was to give $5,000 and take care of our store.

He was a good person. That's how he won my heart. I truly loved him. My first husband was the first man that I loved and there was one other that I loved. Everyone else I loved but I was not in love if I am honest.

I did it to hurt my man, hoping and praying that things would change but that was not the case. I tried to get his attention, but I feel like it turned him against me. So, I said all that to show that I know him very well. Like he knew me.

So, I went to the Steve Harvey comic show. It was nice. I had a good time. I was hoping all of this would come together between the three of us. I had another wife-in-law, but she was not a prostitute. So, it would not have been a good idea. So, he and I had a hotel room for that night. That night we had a good time with the family but that told me everything I needed to know about her.

Square or work square job, a call girl or flat back or work the street or in a sex house, that's what I liked. I liked it more than dancing because I can move like I won monopoly Park Place or Boardwalk or own everything. I can get in my family and man and kids, and just be a help to people. That's another thing I loved about him. He was a giver.

We were planning my welcome home party. So, we were all supposed to get together. My daddy and my wife-in-law. I have an executive suite, a three-bedroom house with a jacuzzi, and room service. Everyone was running around trying to get ready for the party.

We all arrived at the party, but my friend did not call. But she showed up and at that point, I knew we had to do something. Something had to be done but it was up to him what was going to be done because he was the boss. He called the shots. That's how I saw it.

She didn't do what she said she was going to do. So, I took it as if she had changed her mind. I was number one. It didn't matter what everyone tried to make it look like. He did not tell me anything different. So that's what it was. So, let him handle the situation.

I knew at that point he was going to dismiss her because I knew him. He would not put up with that behavior. He did what he needed to do on his own. The day came when he said that was done. They got into his car, but I told him not to worry about people. People always reap what they sew.

Life went on because he was not going to lose what he had for any woman, no matter how good they thought they were to him. He had the best and he was untouchable.

As time went on my life took a turn for the worst because I played paper dancers doing whatever I want to do. I broke every law there was. So, what do you think was going to happen?

I went to prison in 2000 for $280,000. I went down for a 10-year sentence. But my man was there doing everything. He wrote letters and sent cards, beautiful, nice-smelling cards. I had never smelled as many smells and tasted so good. So, I was pleased even knowing he had other women in his life, and for my friend, we did not talk for at least 6 months or more. She went on with her life and I still love her as a friend.

She was not my best friend. When she did find out she stayed in the situation, but I would never have done my best friend like that because I'm her best friend and always will be. Even if she never sees me again. Even when she went with a man a long time before off Portland, she knew him, and I had been together for a very long time. But being the person that I am, I kept on loving her no matter what she had done to me. Anyone else would have been done.

It was because I truly loved her as my best friend, as my sister, but things started to change. I began to see things differently. But I never said anything. I wanted to see how this would play out. I was hurting very bad, but who cared? Did he really care, or did he love me, huh?

I stayed in prison for 18 months. He came out on paper for some years, but he was there for me. He did not wait for me. Waiting is not being involved with other women or not having sex or anything of that nature but continuing in your everyday life until that person is released. Then you come together as a couple. That is what it means to wait.

The word wait means to stay in expectation till the arrival of some person or event. So that is the definition of waiting for someone. I went to Webster's dictionary. So, there it is.

CHAPTER 13
Business, Beatings, and Bad News

I HAD MY own escort service, Mercedes Entertainment. I made good money. I work my own service. I booked my own clients. I had it set up for VIPs, average guys, the rich guys, and the middle class. I had codes they would give me, and I had color codes. One never knew how I work my service.

I had about 200 guys and then I cut it off. I worked out of my own condo. Out of New Hope. Then it got to moving fast and I went to the Brooklyn Center area. I had Super 8, Comfort Inn, Best Western, Crowne

Plaza, Amer Inn, Country Inn, Motel 6, and the Bellmont Hotel. I worked everyone. No more than three nights in the same hotel. No one knew my plans. No friends or no family. No one but my man. So, we had a very good time.

I would cook for my man. He came home on Thursdays, Fridays, and Saturdays. He went over to my wife-in-law on Mondays, Tuesdays, and Wednesdays. Sundays were his day to go over to his friend's home or to just kick it. He would get around. He was not the one to sit in the house. He was a hustler. That was the game, but it was fair.

Life went on and I moved to a big, beautiful apartment with a big swimming pool, big exercise room, and party room. It was so glamorous. I moved so he can have his own bathroom, so we laid that place. It had a garage and free parking space for him. All this time he had another woman that I knew about, so he had his own place. She had her own place. I had my own place too.

So, when he wanted to get together, we got a nice jacuzzi suite. But I had a feeling about it. Could it be possible he has not been honest with me or has not

Chapter 13
Business, Beatings, and Bad News

been as open as he should have been? Anytime a woman is in the bed with her man with four or five different women, what does that say?

First of all, you are a fool, and you can talk to me about anything. It hurt me but I will get over it, but I trust him with my life. I love his son, his grandma, and his father who told him I was a good woman. That if he loses me, he would be a fool. A real man knows a good woman when they see one. I can cook. I was a very clean person. I am a royal, classy woman. I love nice things, nice clothes, and jewelry. I know how to sew and iron.

I had a deep feeling that they lived together and that was not acceptable. He can do what he wanted but not with me. That is a sign of distrust.

So, I started feeling cold-hearted, being a smart mouth, and just being myself. I did not know how to handle it. If this is true, I knew it was going to be over. Eight years gone down the drain. That is so sad.

When they came to the room, they came together with matching suitcases. I was watching things. How he acted and how she acted. Even when I was in bed with him and her, she acted like she did not know how to caress his body or have oral sex. How to just get down freaky from his ears to his hips, from his belly button, down the sides of his legs, down to his toes back to his you know what. Lick up and down. Make love to his mind not his body.

Over and over for at least 3 hours, then they do you the same way. Making all kinds of sounds, taking short breaths, until you feel your heart about to stop. Reaching the peak was awesome. Taking turns Sixty-nine on each other. Then I made love to her, the same way I made love to him. That was the best oral sex because I had been with a woman most of my life and had more oral sex with women.

The Beatdown

We went to a bar called Catch. On the way, I'm just a high-class prostitute. When we got to the door, this lady did not want to let me in. So, my man and her got through the door, and so did I. They got all the way in, I did not.

I thought as him being my man, he would go and get the owner because I knew him very well. He was my ex-boyfriend, and I was a good person. He knew my lifestyle and he looked up to me. But, instead of

Chapter 13
Business, Beatings, and Bad News

getting him, he went in like I didn't belong to him. I had someone to get him, and he came and let me in and told the lady to stop hating on me.

When I got inside, I had a drink. I thought about all that happen, and I went off. He was very embarrassed. I call him out, but I did not think that it was that bad. But I was not listening to me either. So, I wanted to leave. I felt bad that I had acted that way in front of everyone. As soon as we entered the room all eyes were on us. So, I just wanted to leave.

The best thing was to leave, or he is going to beat me for real. So, we left. She got in first, he got in second and I got in third. I went off in the car and hit him. He hit me back and start hitting me like I was a man. Like he never knew me.

I started fighting him back. He pulled my hair out in the top and that was the thing he shouldn't ever have done to me. I picked up my phone like I was going to call the police. I wanted him to think I was and pushed the number. He hit me and the phone hit the floor. When we got to the hotel and made it to the room, we started to argue. The people heard us and called the police because things do happen at this kind of hotel.

He wanted to say I called the police on him. He had some green and he had some smoke. Before we left and they saw the ashtray and fined us $200. I had paid for the room on a credit, but it was not going to go through until we check-in. I was supposed to be the one to do that for his birthday.

The police came and I left the room. I wanted my truck and my keys that I let him drive. We would take turns driving it, but he just acted like I bought it for him. But if I did, I would not be driving it because it was for him.

Bad News

We had a very good time in Kansas City. We went on shopping sprees just for him and got whatever he wanted. He could have had anything he wanted but I gave him what he asked for. He never said to me I wanted a Mercedes-Benz, or Rolls-Royce and the reason I never just surprised him on my own was that first of all, when he went to pick a woman, he picked a square. So, I treat him like a square. That's how I felt. He never said something was wrong.

Her and I would meet over at his house to clean it and she had keys, but I gave him more than she ever could. So, I knew right then I was right. The time was right to find out what was really going on with the man I love. So, I knew my heart would not be broken. So, his 50th birthday was coming up on November 29th and we had plans to have a threesome. We did Friday night and Saturday night was his birthday. We had it for the weekend.

He asked me for jewelry, whatever it was, I tried to help his whole family if I could. I love all his kids, but his son was my son. He was my favorite and still is. He is the son I never had. As the night went on, I got him a Bentley, all white and golden inside.

I noticed his car was parked when I got to the car. So, I took off. All he wanted was the truck. That's all. So, I took him to the truck and went on about my business. I continued to work. I had six felony warrants. I knew I'm getting ready to do something. So, I call him.

As I was riding one day, I got up the nerve to ask him what I wanted to ask him after all these years, did he live with her? He said, "Yes".

I was so hurt. So, I turned around off the freeway and onto another freeway and home. At that time, while I'm still talking to him on the phone, I wanted to know why he would do this to me after all I had done for him.

We had been a family all this time. But he let someone come between us. What had happened? He fell in love with her. That was the bottom line, but he was not man enough to tell me how he really felt. At that point, it was over. I know I had done my best, but I guess I was never good enough. I was just a meal ticket for him.

So, he wanted her to drive his Cadillac, he drove the Denali XL, and I drove the Bentley. So that told me about him. I realized I didn't know this man at all. He showed his true colors. So, I left the hotel, called for a ride, and they came and got me.

Before I left, I called AAA to come and tow the truck. He didn't come out to see if I was okay or if I got a ride. He just locked the door behind me. I'm the one that plan all of this, so he showed me he really didn't care for me. I had to get out of this mess. But I went on with his party, had his sex, and let him do what he wanted to do.

Chapter 13
Business, Beatings, and Bad News

The next morning, while I was still sleeping, she called me talking about that's done. I said, "That's not my problem anymore". I was done with this mess.

I guess they got a ride somehow. I never asked because I did not care. He came to my girl's house looking for me. So, I knew he got out and he walked through the house.

He would not have done that to my house. If I did not want you there, you were not going to take over my house. He left. She told him I was there. So, he called later and said it was a bad storm. He said that his car didn't work. What do you expect? It was a Cadillac, not a Mercedes-Benz.

Dinner in Prison

On one occasion, when I was in prison, the Holy Spirit spoke to me and said for Him to bring unity there. This was the worse unit. I begin to pray and fast, be set apart and he spoke again, and He gave me the mindset to do it. When God tells you to do something. He would guide you all the way through.

So, the word got out about what God wanted me to do. Give a dinner. He knew how to do it because he knew what was in their minds. He made them, so he knows what to do.

I was in IFI. It was a Christian base, and I was studying the bible for at least 5 hours a day, 5 days a week. The CO did not believe in Christ. But God said it would be done even if I got to the hole.

So, I called and told my family about what was going on and to keep me in their prayers. I felt good about it. I knew it was God that spoke to me.

So, me and my IFI sister got together. I did not get any support from my teacher or the person that was over IFI. So right there, that told me that the people in prison were afraid of what might happen. They might lose their job.

So, they would tell me, that if Jesus spoke to them, they would be afraid of the prison CO that worked there. But what we need to understand is we are the body of Christ. We are one body and when we are commanded to do something by God, we need to know that He is the highest authority. He is the high priest, and I cannot wait to see God's face.

I started ordering food, drinks, and everything that we could eat. We made pizza, tamales, and burritos.

We had enough to feed 170 people. God moved. It was awesome.

The Lord was in the prison, and I felt the spirit moving. The COs, Tucker and Travis, were so moved in their heart. People in their rooms that could not come out, or those that were sick, or those that had gotten written up, God made sure they got fed. It was so awesome. Everyone got fed.

I ate last. All that helped, I let them get what they wanted. We shared. We had food left for three days. God is good, all the time. Everyone on the grounds heard about it. They said that they wish they would have been there. To God be the glory. God did get the glory out of it.

But here comes Satan, trying to take me to the hole. Nothing happened. She submitted the paperwork. No weapon formed against me shall prosper, in Jesus name. Blessing be to God. There were lots of witnesses.

It never was the same and never will be the same in Shakopee Prison. I love my sisters in there and the warden. She is a nice lady and things were changing in that place. It is very hard to change because people keep coming back which is making it a little different in that place.

On another occasion, I had gone to the grocery store and shopping, and when I came off the highway, I came to the stop sign. I paused but did not make a complete stop. The police put the lights on me, and I pulled over.

I proceeded to give him my insurance card and driver's license. I was driving my gold Jaguar V8 S-Type and I had a feeling that I was going to jail one way or another, so I called my sister. The police said I had a warrant, and it was a $20,000 bail. So, I went to jail.

Before I got there, they said there was nothing going on. After I had been there for a while, not even an hour, God spoke to me and said, "There people are going home today." So, I spoke and the three included me. I left in three hours and went home. Some of the other girls too.

God worked through me. God moved in that place and the CO said he had never seen anything like this. He said that it was very good. God be glorified. I thank you for everything that you have done and will do, in Jesus name.

I don't have a mind like the mind I had before. My old mind was always of the world. So, when I think spiritually, God is at work. My mind is no longer my mind but His mind.

I want to be like Jesus. Why? Because he is perfect, righteous, holy, peaceful, joyful, and faithful, and he does not lie. He is the son of the living God. Who in the right mind would not want to be like Jesus? I must be like him.

I wonder what it feels like to not sin, to do everything right, walk right, look right, to say everything that is right. Oh God, help my mind to understand your will and your ways. Lord, come bring light when I walk in the room. Let it light up like the sun. God, I feel the spirit move on me.

I do not have the desire to be like anyone in the body of Christ. I only want to be whom God has called me to be. I know all the hell I have been through. I know it is greatness. To whom much is given, much is required.

I don't have a man. Yes, it gets lonely. Yes, I'm tired of sleeping by myself and I want a mate. But I can wait through Christ Jesus who strengthens me. He is able to keep me from falling.

Oh God, send your Holy Spirit to help me. I plead the blood of Jesus over my mind, heart, and soul. Lord, you said in Isaiah 41:12-13, you might search for your enemies, but you will not find them. Those who go to war against you will completely disappear. I am the Lord your God. I take hold of your right hand. I say to you, do not be afraid I will help you. You are the holy one of Israel.

Jesus, you are faithful, holy, and righteous. You are so perfect. God make me just like Jesus. Make me to think like him and walk like him. Make my heart like his heart. O God, make my knowledge just like Jesus. I want to not sin at all. Make me all over again. Cleanse me, purify me, make me whole Lord. Let your will be done in me.

CHAPTER 14
Some of the Hardest
Things I've Done

I WAS ASKING God what he wanted me to say, and the spirit took me up. He used me like never before. I saw everybody get up and jump up and down. I heard a loud noise, and I was like, "My God, what is going on?" The Spirit said, "I got you. Just keep going."

I was moved and everyone else spoke and it was so awesome. She had a very good homegoing. So, I was good, and the Holy Spirit started on my daughter. God started using her. She was a prophesying. After all of that, everyone gathered to eat. The woman of God called me. The film director, and producer wanted to film me and fifteen women at Shiloh Temple Church. God moved in me that day. All glory to God.

In another instance, God had me go to the hospital and pray for this woman. It was my hair designer's mom. The Holy Spirit told me what to do. I went to her room with my Bible and my Holy oil. Prayed her room up, anointed her room, and her pillow, and believe in God to do what he started in me.

The Holy Spirit told me to pray for her and to speak to her mind because Satan was trying to take her mind. I prayed and prayed, and the Holy Spirit said, "Maudell, you don't know who this is. She is a mighty woman of God. Give her the word and God said, "She will speak to millions". I said, "Wow".

We drove off and God's mission was complete. I went home and my life took off like a jet. He had not put me in a rope yet. So, I continued to move for the Lord.

The very first platform I spoke on was at Shiloh Temple, West Broadway, Minneapolis, Minnesota. It was a celebration for my girl who had passed away. She was born and raised in Chicago, Illinois. We stayed around the corner from each other. Her family had not seen me in a long time. They were surprised by what they saw.

I had on a Christian robe and God's glory was upon me. I heard from the Holy Spirit, that her kids wanted me to speak but somehow, I was not on it. So, I told the pastor what God said, and he said, "Your name is not on it but I'm going to put your name on it."

My daughter and I were seated in the front, and the man came up and took my hand and helped me onto the platform and seated me in my seat. God went before me and prepared the way for me. I was so moved in my spirit.

Then we left them, it was the last day. It was a blessing. We checked out of the hotel. The Holy Spirit spoke again and said, "I want you to go to Waycross, Georgia.". So, I went.

I stayed at a friend's house. We got there, we went to sleep, then got up the next morning. We prayed and prayed, and the Spirit moved. I stayed there for 30 days waiting for God to tell me what he wanted me to do.

I had to fly home. I had a closing to do and then I flew back to Waycross. Then God spoke to my friend, and she said, "God wants you to go down to Oakdale Street where the pimps, prostitutes, homosexuals, hustlers, players, and drug dealers are". My friend drove my Hummer. I sat in the passenger side.

When we got there a woman walked out of the bar and walk straight to the truck. She knew my friend. I could see in the spirit how God had set it up. I began to prophesy to her and tell her everything the Holy Spirit was telling me.

Deliverance took place. God was in that place. The Holy Spirit led me. He led me to go and pray for a pastor that I knew and his wife. They were very close. He had cancer. I was there at his wedding, and it was very beautiful. This is when they needed me the most.

We went to the hospital and prayed and laid hands. We were waiting for God to move. I left and went home the next day. His wife called and invited me for dinner. I went and I remembered talking to Pastor Shultz.

He told me, "If I die, Satan will never get the glory from me, only God. Please be there for my wife". I said, "I will do what I can". After that, I left and flew

Chapter 14
Some of the Hardest Things I've Done

to Orlando, Florida. My daughter, grandkids, and son-in-law came to pick me up.

I spent a week in Orlando. It was very nice. But I got a call when I got back in town and now, I was being hit with a double take. Pastor was in the hospital and Jackie's was too and it did not look good.

I got dressed, put on my robe, got my bible, and holy oil, and began to pray, and allow the Holy Spirit to move in his life and in my spirit. I started to praise God and sing songs and lift up the name of Jesus.

Within 48 hours she was at the house, and it was unreal. The Holy Spirit moved. He just used me. He just needs a body to be holy and willing to do God's will. He showed me who I am in Christ Jesus. I went back to Iowa, to my church that I had joined when I got out of prison and got baptized. Then I left there and went back the Minnesota where I'm from.

My sister came with me, and a few ministers and prophets came as well. I fasted and prayed, and they drove me. We got there and checked into our hotel and rested for the day.

God woke us up and we got ready to go to see what God has for his people. We went and I studied and prayed that the Spirit leads me, and my flesh would die. We made it to the church and were seated. When they called my name, the Holy Spirit said, "You will not be needing that paper". I obeyed the spirit and God move like never before. He used my sister as well. It was all God.

They invited us to come back to preach the word of God. They did go back, and I went back with them. They preached on love and my other sister preached on Job. It was a blessing.

We picked up his mom and his wife. We went to the hospital, and we went in. He was in a deep sleep. Now, I was on the same floor with both of them and I had been praying my heart out to God. Just pouring it out. Having faith, no matter what it looked like.

So, I kept my head up. They were one room over from each other, so I would go from room to room and pray and pray. But they had bought bad news for Pastor sweet and said he will not make it.

His mom and his wife said they cannot take it. They asked me to be with him. I thank God that he allowed me to come at such a time. I read Psalm 121,

Psalms 23, and Psalms 27, as those were his favorite scriptures. I did not know that.

I prayed with him, and it was for 55 minutes until he took his last breath, and I lost it. I was so hurt, but I still had to control myself and know who is in control. God said to me, "You did what you were supposed to do. I call him home. I'm God."

I was at peace with it. I called his wife and told her when he died. She needed to get there quickly, and she said that they are not that far away.

That was one of the hardest things I ever had to do. My heart was crushed into millions of pieces. His mom lost it and his wife and then the kids came. People came, the pastor came, and they got their last look. His wife closed her eyes.

It was so sad, but we knew he was with the Lord where he wanted to be. So, we went to his house and stayed there with his wife and mom, and family. It was very quick, and we could not eat or sleep. Morning came and we began to rejoice in the Lord.

The Holy Spirit Moving through Me

So, I went to this church to hear the word of God and God had a robe me then and I went with my sister.

This preacher was bringing the word of God. We started to praise the Lord and give honor to him and to the Holy Spirit. The man of God spoke prophecies to them, and I did too.

Then the Holy Spirit came over me and took over and it was awesome. The Holy Spirit told me to double portion, and I laid hands on them, then the Holy Spirit took over in the name of Jesus. I was a little shaken up so because I knew I did not do that, and I was right. The Holy Ghost took over and they were laid on the floor. Husband and wife. God moved in their lives, and it was awesome.

I was in the church praising the Lord and I got so many prophecies from the prophet. The Holy Spirit spoke to them to tell me my husband is coming. He never said when. These are all different times and ministries. He also prophesied that my family would come together, and another prophetess spirit spoke through and gave me instructions when I get to Florida and what to do and what not to do.

He talked about me being a general and I move in deliverance. It was prophesied over my life that I would bring demons out of people, pimps, sexual acts, homosexuals, prostitutes, out of prison, drug dealers, players, gangs, death row, murderers, lawyers, judges, prosecutors, high priests, false teachers, false preachers, women of have been raped, been on drugs, lust spirits, lying spirits, controlling. Everything that is not of God.

It was prophesied I would prophesy into people's lives, that God is bringing me to the forefront on the lines and many I don't have to lay hands on, just walk past them and they will be healed and delivered. I will go out of the country, go into prison, will be ordained and licensed, and keep my robe on until my husband comes, then I will only wear it when I minister.

The Holy Spirit spoke and said what kind of mansion I will have built from the ground. I will not owe any money on it, just property taxes. He told me how it's supposed to be built. Very detailed. He told me the kinds of exotic cars I will have and how my jet was supposed to look. It will have 12 seats, white on the outside and inside a gold bed.

He told me when my husband comes, he is going to take over and have control over my ministries. He's going to fire and hire people. Some will go and some will stay. I'm supposed to let him do what God has called him to do. He is supposed to be approved by my leaders, so we cannot and will not go wrong. Only God will be in it. Satan has nothing to offer me. He's the same devil.

The spirit told me and others what is to come. When a prophecy is to come it doesn't mean right now. The only way it will be is if it is in God's will. If it is a right now word, it's because he can do a quick work in anyone he pleases because he is God. He is the creator, the first and the last, the beginning and the end, he's the alpha and the omega. He is the root of David, he is the father of Abraham, Isaac, and Jacob. He is the same god that raised Jesus from the dead.

It's Over

So, I went home and packed my suitcase. He tried to talk to me, but I was not hearing anything he had to say to me. I kept packing my clothes and he kept trying to talk to me. He kept going until I finished. I said to him it was over and you can have her. You and her can go to hell.

I packed my car and told him he can have everything in the house. I jumped in my car and left. For a while, I cried a little on the way to Houston,

Chapter 14
Some of the Hardest Things I've Done

Texas. I took Highway 35 South all the way to Beaumont, then it changes to 45 South all the way into Houston. I got a hotel.

I did not know what I was going to do. One thing, I had my you know what and it was very good. I can sell it anywhere in the world. Even at the North Pole, it would be okay. So, when I got checked into a hotel. I stayed there to get the entertainment guide to look for escort services. I started talking to other girls. Beaunette was the strip where hookers hang and make money.

So, I was working the streets for a while, then this show where the massage parlor was, and I got in. Then I got a job in one of the Gallery Mall right by there, I left Minnesota.

My ex-man said that when I get there, call him. But I was not thinking about him at that time. I was hurt. I never felt so betrayed. He and I were better. I did tell another one of my sugar daddies I was going to give him a chance. Through this, we will be together. I would stand by my word. So, I stayed there for 11 months. During that time, I was looking through the guide for some work.

I saw this very beautiful woman and she was hot as hell. She looked like a black Barbie, and I mean hot. I called the number, and she answered the phone. She met me at my hotel room.

She knocked on my door and open the door. It was her. When she walked in, she looked just like she did in the guide. I noticed she had the biggest ad in the paper. I knew she made good money.

She was talking to me, asking me questions about who I was. I was straight up. I told her all that I knew about the game, that I had knowledge of the game, and that I had a mouthpiece. She and I together can make it. She knew the town and I had the knowledge, the body, and the look, and she was hot on hot. Beautiful. We could catch any bees with our honey.

I had it all together, this is how we can make some money. About $25,000 in two days. So, we did. I told her this was my real name, and no one should ever know it, no matter what happens. She said, "Okay". I also told her I had six felony warrants and I told her why. She said, "Okay, let's do this" and we did.

She went to talk to her man about it and an apartment. We went and picked it out. He went to get it and we got furniture. We got everything together and had it set up for VI Pony, and things started to happen. We really started to get to know each other. I felt like I could trust her.

Time went on and I went to meet her man. I thought he was a pimp, but he was not. He had his own insurance agency. So, I stayed over there until everything went through about the condo.

They cooked for me. I met her mom, her father, and her little brother. His family was so nice, and I liked them. They tried nothing with me, and they treated me like family. I honored that. I really did.

So, we finished moving. We went half on everything. We made so much money, but it was like the Midwest, it was so different. So, I kept that in the back of my head.

We started to shake and move some things. We went out to high-class places, so we did okay. But I knew I had a warrant, so I was not myself, but I tried to do my best.

We were doing good, and my birthday was coming up on July 16th. My man had never missed my birthday. So, he called and said I need to come home to take care of my warrant. I told him, don't worry about me, I was good. But he said my birthday is coming and I want to see you.

He would go anywhere to see me. So, he drove and made it the day of my birthday. My friend and I met him. It seemed as if he was glad to see me. He hugged me and I hugged and kissed him. I missed him so much. I couldn't eat or sleep, I lost weight. I was going to lose my mind. I took him to our house and got him some grass hydedro. The best. So, he unpacked.

I bought myself a Suzie for my birthday. He named it "Daddy Boy Harbin". He took me out to Joe's Crab shack. It was so nice. I wanted my man back, but I could not get past the pain I was feeling. Yes, I was still so, so, in love with him but I set my feelings aside because I know I did not mean that much to him. I was just some sex and money, and that was it.

He stayed for some weeks and my feelings kept coming back. I was hurting so bad. For 3 weeks I hurt. It was all coming back so, I went to work for the week, and I called him and said, "By the time I get home you can leave. It is not going to work with us."

Chapter 14
Some of the Hardest Things I've Done

When I got there, he had packed his clothes in the truck. He went to take the dog outside and then he came back to give me a hug. He took off and I fell to the floor. Crying and hollering as loud as I could cry.

I cried and cried until I could not cry anymore. I didn't eat. I was so lost because all these years I had never been without him. I couldn't sleep. I had dreams because I always wanted to be his wife. I always wanted a big, beautiful wedding and to be retired from the game.

I was qualified to be with him and marry him. It happened all the time in the game. But I guess I wasn't what he wanted. So, I let it go. I don't want anyone that does not want me, and I was okay with all that.

So, I'll call Nathan. He sent me a cell phone. That was when he was really a pimp. But I didn't do anything with him because I had given my man my word.

CHAPTER 15
In and Out of Prison, But God…

I GOT ARRESTED in 1999. I bonded out. I was out for one year, and that gave me time to get myself together. I was thankful to God for that. I had to turn myself in and I did. I went to court, and they did give me 10 years. If I turned some of the money in, they would try to get me three to five years.

So, we worked that out with the prosecutor and the judge. That was the least I could get for the crime I committed. Before I went, my sister told me everything God had told her about me and what was going to happen before I ever got there. That is called a prophecy.

So, I left, and I got there, and they took me to Oakdale for 4 weeks. Oakdale is where you had to go before you go to the main prison. I stayed there until they came to get me.

So, my day came for me to leave Oakdale and when I got to the prison, it was like nothing I had ever seen in my life. It was unreal but it was so real. Then I went to get changed out, get settled in, and then to my room. I got all set up and went to the admit building. I had to go do some paperwork.

As I was going, I heard someone say, "Kat". That was the name I used for 16 years of my life. It was my friend that I knew on the outside. She asked me why I was there, and I did the same. We met outside and talked. She was there for murder, and I had to hear about Tobias but she did not understand what I was saying. She had set a house on fire, and someone was killed.

She told everyone that I was her friend and that if I had any problem with anyone, for them to take care of it because they had life and I had to go and preach the word of God. They said, "Okay" and they had my back. I got a job at a manufacturing company. I got $170 every week.

So, I was just walking outside listening to my radio, power walking around, and this lady was trying to get my attention. I stopped to see what she wanted, and she asked me my name and I said, "Mercedes". She said can she asked me why I was there, and I said, "Theft in the first degree, and I got 10 years". She said you be out of here in no time and she said your time was cut in half when you walk through the door.

She said you'll do 11 months on a 10-year sentence. She said she had 100 years and I said, "What!" She said, "I had an ounce of cocaine, and I had a gun it was not a murder weapon" and she had a joint of grass and that was it. I asked her, "Do you believe in Jesus Christ?" She said, "Yes".

So, I began to pray for her, and I said to her, "God will move in your life in the name of Jesus. Meet me out here every day" and she did. Her name was May. Every day for about one month we met, and God spoke to me and said to tell her, "It is done". So, I told her what God said and 90 days later she left. She won her appeal.

So, everybody wanted me to pray. What they wanted to do was prostitute my gifts and God is not having that. I went to work every morning and to school. Every day was the same. The parole board came once a year and you had to be on your best behavior. If you've been good for a whole year then suddenly you get a ticket or write-up, then you have to wait until the next year.

Then I met another girl. She was a white girl. Size three, long beautiful hair, brunette, pretty face, and a very good attitude. She had a very good personality, but she was involved with another girl.

She was fed up with her and wanted to get with me. But I had one of the best reports on the ground. So, I had this girl that had a bad report, so it made it known to everyone that she and I were together, let everybody know what was up.

So, as time went on, and I prayed for people because God allowed me to do so. I know I cannot do anything without God. I cannot breathe, sleep, eat, speak, see, feel, touch, cannot move without my God, the living God. Jesus is the son of God. Lord, I think you.

Things went on and I was going to church. One of the ladies said to me, "Stand up". At that time, I had been thinking about singing. If God gives me my voice back, I will sing for him. She said to me, "Stand up" and she said, "God said put together a choir". I was thinking, how am I going to do that? She said, "Just do it".

I begin to ask everyone if they wanted to be in the choir and God got a 35-person choir together, including me. He put together the choir and every important person was there in the community. It was a sight to see.

Everyone was so emotional and crying and singing for the Lord. Oh God! This was never seen before. The whole prison was there. God put it together. He is so awesome.

God's ways are not our ways. His thoughts are not like our thoughts. He is so different. I just want to learn about him, His son, and the Holy Spirit, and that is by the word of God and through the Holy Spirit. By hearing the word of God, when you and I obey the word of God, He will move mountains.

I'm understanding a little spot. I think Jesus for going to the cross to die for our sins. Can you imagine someone dying for your sins without a spot or blemish? Oh, God! This is something I cannot even wrap my mind around, what it meant to him. Oh my God, please help me to understand your way and your thoughts.

After that, everyone I prayed for, God blessed. Then the people from parole came and I got my freedom in 5 minutes. Mrs. G. Frances said to me, "I better not ever see you again" and she has not. I left, went home, and started my life back. Praise God in everything you do, amen.

Iowa Prison

In 2003, I was back in prison for a violation. I was back in prison, in green, and in the hole. It was the first time in my life I had been in the hole, and throughout my prison sentences, this was the worst thing that could ever happen to me. But God was not done with me.

I started reading, Rick Warren. My life changed totally after reading it. Like God himself wrote the book. No human could have ever written that without the Holy Spirit, amen. I was sitting in my cell, and something came over me. Lord, help me. I felt like something was wrong. I felt different. I was thinking differently. It was very, very, strange but I could not put my hands on it.

Time went on, and that's when God came to me and said, "You don't believe the Holy Spirit lives in you." I was lying down and a thick cloud of smoke in the form of a snake came from my window. It came toward me and down in my stomach and went through my stomach. I jumped up and looked around.

I stayed there for 199 days and was then released to work release. I had to stay for nine months. They wanted me to discharge my number so, in the process of that, God moved in that place like never before. He was using me, and I prayed and prayed like never before, and everything that I prayed for happened.

God allowed me to lay the seed, but he is the only one to make it grow. He is the Almighty, the beginning and the end, the Alpha, and the Omega, He is the root and the son of David. He is the bright and morning star.

Right in the women's correction center, I knew something was going on with me. I was not understanding what was going on and it was not me. I saw things in a way I never had before. Oh, my Lord, God! What is it? Jesus, help me. Give me the strength to go on. Holy Spirit come to me because you are the action and the teacher and the trainer. Thank you for what you are doing but I don't think I'm qualified for this.

I'm a sinner that is saved by grace and mercy. Cover me in the blood of Jesus. Holy, holy, holy. You are holy, amen.

Still Making Moves

I had promised one of my sugar daddies, that when I got totally free, I would give him a chance just to see what he is about. So, once I was out and back in Minnesota, I went to his cell store to see if he is there, but his brother was in there. He was off that day. His brother told me he would be in tomorrow. I said, "Okay"

When I walked in the next day, he said, "Hey baby how are you?" I said, "Good." He said, "Why you did not call me baby?" I said, "I forgot your last four digits. But I'm here now. By the way, remember when we had that talk about us getting together?" He looked at me so surprised. He said, "For real baby?" I said, "Yes".

We left and got in this Mercedes and took off. We went and had lunch to talk about some things. Everything we needed we talk about to get an understanding. To make sure we are on the right track. In a day or two, we had to go shopping. He bought me everything I needed.

We spent time together, getting to know each other, and in the next two days, and then I was on my way. I went to the casino, and I went to Las Vegas to work at Cherry Patch. It was okay but not at all like I was making money in Elko, Nevada. This is a complete turnaround. I stayed for 2 weeks and then went on the strip and made some moves and had some clients.

He kept me in the hotel. We spent lots of time together there. That was in 2003. I was playing paper. My friend was around me at that time, so it was good.

I had always made moves by myself, so I would not have anyone telling me anything. If we got caught or messed it up, it takes a long time to print for them.

Making and printing it take one check, it takes six to seven hours so no one could ever be there but me and him.

So, as life went on, I had to pay $280,000 at this bank. The time came for me to go to court, and it all came up, so I was dealing with something, so I went to prison in 2000 for that charge. I had got a case for forgery, so I went to jail, and he came to put money on my book. From there I went to prison, and he was there for me, and money was not a problem. I was very comfortable, I was good, and I knew everyone in the prison.

I had gone to prison before, so I was okay. I went to church, worked out, prayed, and signed up for classes. First, I have to be honest about everything from the front to the back. I must be truthful and honest about everything I'm saying and writing about. The only reason I got with him is to make my ex mad. I hoped he would change his ways.

I thought that he would come to me, talk to me, and try to get back together. But in my heart, I knew that it was over, but I never stopped trying because I did love him. I never liked Charles in that way, but Charles grew on me.

So, time went on and they transferred me from Minnesota to Iowa. To prison in Midfield Iowa for a 10-year sentence. But God's grace and his mercy covered me. I think Jesus.

Since I had a violation, I did 199 days in the hole. It was not a good thing. It was punishment. That's when the Holy Spirit came down on me in a white cloud. I was reading Purpose Driven Life by Rick Warren and every question I had for God was answered through the book.

So, I did 40 days, and the book was real to me. God was really talking to me through this book, and it changed my life forever. But I had a long way to go before I would get where God was taking me. Oh my! So, I was fasting for 30 days. Liquid only. So, I did that time, and I was released to the Correction Center for 9 months.

Time went on, so I call him and said, "If you don't have a car up here on Sunday, I was done". He can keep going. So, he knew I was very serious about it. He came and I got a room at the hotel, and he spent a little time with me. He bought the car up and I went back to work release, checked back in, and we talked.

They tried to stop me from praising the Lord. I prayed for every woman in the place and in every prayer that I prayed for them, it happened. It was awesome. The people were following me, day in and day out. God was moving in that place, and they were trying to send me back to prison.

But God was good through it all and I love him. So, we should obey him or else we are liars. I don't want to be a liar in God's eyes. That's all that matters to me. What God thinks.

I had to wait to be discharged. I had to be patient and let go and let God. I worked two jobs to stay out of that place. My day would come. He came to see me until I got out. He was there for me. He put money on my phone, up to $300. He sent me money. He spent $5,000 on me in prison but I left him with $30,000.

Time went on and I can honestly say, he was good to me and spent money on me all the time. He was a gentleman and treated me like the woman that I am. He was so good to me, and I like the way he talked, and he told me about his baby's mom. He was with her for 14 and 1/2 years and his other women.

So, I asked him if he was married, and he said no. I respected what he said and if he was, I would have still been with him. It did not matter. I stayed with him, and I was truly a lady in the game, and he had to pimp or die. If you were not down with me all the way, you had to go. For real.

So, life went on and he and I put some things together. What I loved about him was he was a business-minded man, which I have never had. I was used to being the one that was putting it all together, buying everything, and making the money.

Now here he comes, and I was happy to have someone who had their own business. I love making money, at least in some legal way. So, he was no different from any other man.

So, I was starting to make some real money. He said that he knew a place in Montana. We called and she booked me.

I went down there for a month. I made a lot of money, and we pulled around $30,000 out of that place. Yes, I gave him money, but I kept what I needed. We had a good understanding. I came back to Minnesota, and three days later, he sent me to Las Vegas to work back at the Cherry Patch. This time it was different. It was more and more of the owner's own women and his personnel.

I was making money, but he had changed. He wanted to pay for things we normally do in the house. Let them make all the money. He would get a lot of it. So, you had to know how the game goes. It is just like the people in the world. So, I was getting upset. No matter how hard I try he would still make sure they got the guys.

I did not try to figure it out. I just talk to my man about it. He said, "Just hang in there, baby. By the way, how do you feel if send someone down there with you? You keep your eyes on her and see who she talking to on the phone. See how much money she makes and stay sweet. I love you honey". I said "Okay Daddy. Talk to you later" and I did everything he asked me to do.

Time went on and I was still in love with one of my sugar daddies. Even as I write this book. I can be very honest about it, but I will be okay. I have to let things go with him. I don't want to even fight with him. So, I let it all go so I can do what God wants me to do, amen.

Time went on and the girl came there, and she was very young and pretty but always thought that I was bad and cold. Anyway, it worked out well. I made sure what she didn't have, I had it. So, it was good.

We talked. I tried not to say anything that would hurt or change her mind about anything or say anything about him because there was too much to say. At that time, I was more and more about my money than about him.

But feelings were getting involved and I let my guard down a little. But I knew where my heart was, so I was dealing with the new life I was trying to deal with, but I missed my ex-man. I could not sleep at night and many nights I could not eat or think. All I thought about was who he was with. I missed looking at him and I missed talking to him, holding him, and making love to him. We were down and dirty with it.

But I still stayed and tried to work it. He had at least 10 in his pocket. When I got home, he showed me the money I had first given him. That was $25,000.

It was the same money. So, I said, "Okay baby, let's do this". Charles was okay with us leaving the house and going to the strip in Vegas to get a room.

I went and found a room for us. I took a shower, got dressed, and we went to the strip. We went to Riviera to work, then I met the pit boss. He was hot.

I was trying to stack thousands after thousands. My sugar daddy said I had gotten too old, but my money let it be known, you have one of the best. But I wondered why he didn't know how to apply himself to get what he wanted out of me. It was very simple. I want this, can you help me, baby? That's what a pimp says.

I need $50,000, you think you can make it happen? I will do my best daddy. It's that simple because I was in it to win it. But he just did not get it, but I gave him only what he asked for. I did not really want to be with him anymore. But I was in love with him and did not know how to get past it.

CHAPTER 16
I'm Done with This

I WAS STANDING by this guy, and I wanted all the money he had in chips, $20,000. If I can get him away from the table and take him to the room, then I have everything he has. I'll get on the plane and go home and start over. That was what I was trying to accomplish. but I didn't get him away from the table. I told him where I was staying and I was going to go ahead of him, so didn't look funny. I will see you there.

At that time, I did not have the time to explain what was going on to the girl working with me. She should have known automatically what was going to happen. This is what you get when you try to be in the game without knowledge and boss sense. You will mess everything up.

I left, went to the room, and waited for him. She shows up, my wife-in-law. She was angry that I left her. Now, if she knew the game, she would have been trying to make some money, instead of worrying about where I went and about daddy's business.

She was at the room, knocking on the door, and talking very loudly. Everyone in the parking lot of the hotel can hear her. I'm thinking about this trick is on his way with $20,000 and she is banging on the door. So, I got very angry.

I knew when she shows up, it was not going to be funny. I open the door and beat her down until it felt good. The trick showed up in a cab and left very quickly. She called the police on me, and they took me to jail. They had me on a 72-hour hold. It was so cold in there.

Then, I got a phone call. He knew I was in jail. My bond was $3,000, but I told him to wait to see if they were going to let me go. We did and they let me out.

Chapter 16
I'm Done with This

So, now I was so upset about the girl. Now, I have an assault on my record. So, he bought me a plane ticket to come home. I got home, jumped in my Mercedes, and was still on top of my money.

I had a court date, so I had to fly to Vegas for court. They dropped the charges against me. That was very good. But I had a warrant. So, I could not go back to the legal sex house in Vegas because you cannot have a warrant. So, now I have to work in an illegal house. So, I got some more work to make money. I worked at the casinos and Shakopee Mystic Lake. I worked there for over 15 years because that's the way I met him. He was playing blackjack with about $30, 000.

I had never had a black trick before. My friend knew him, and he tried to talk to me. I said, "Hello". He asked me, "What's your name?" I said, "I can't talk". Me and my friend went to the girl's room, and she told me about him and his baby's mom.

I was still with Samuel when I met him. I couldn't have anything to do with him and because I told you I was still in love with Samuel. But if I ever got free I would talk to him. That was it.

The next day I went by his store. He knew what was going on and at that time my man passed by and saw my truck outside. He asked me about it. I just said I was buying a phone. He knew I was telling a lie and I did not lie to him about anything. But that was my way to leave him. That's why I felt like I could go out to lunch with Charles.

I left Samuel went to Texas. I came back in 11 months and got with my new man for good. At least for right now. Time went on and I moved around. We spent time together, and went out to dinner, to the movies, and to the fitness center. I was enjoying my life.

We were getting ready to go to Detroit for the Super Bowl. I was shopping, I went to the bank, and I drew out $8,000. I had my niece draw $5,000. They called the police, and they took me to the police station. They called to verify the checks. But I was good to go because I knew it was right. I had not done anything wrong. They took me back to my car.

I got in my car and drove off to go to see my man so we can pack. We took off. Started traveling and we stop in Windy City. I got a room in Fort Point

Chapter 16
I'm Done with This

Sheraton. We had a very good time. We left and started off to Detroit Michigan. It was a time I would never forget.

When we got there, I had a call. I was working the service. Before I got there so many men were talking to me on my cell. We were shaking and moving all around the city. We were happy and got ready to go to the Motown Casino and to the End Zone to eat. I had greens, cornbread, sweet potatoes, and perch fish for 9 days straight. We took calls the whole time.

We set in the VIP section and watch the game. We lost but we celebrated. We had a very good time. Now it was nighttime, and it was time to make the most money. I was sharp and the men were looking at me saying, "Who is that sexy chocolate woman."

I set at the blackjack table and cashed $5,000. My man never knew how I got that money. It was very funny because he claims to have all this street knowledge and he could not even tell me what I had done.

So, we stayed there after the super bowl was over. He took me shopping. We spent some money. We had the time of our lives. We had sex seven days in a row.

We could not keep our hands off each other. It was good.

We left and went back to Chicago. Got a room and went shopping and had a good time. We then went over to Hammond Indiana to the Horseshoes Casino. I got money there and everywhere we went. We had a good time and got thousands. Then we went back to our room and got some rest so we can drive back to Minnesota.

We stopped at the casino, and he gambled. I watched him make some money. He was very good at gambling. He played cards, dice, or poker. Whatever he played he was a winner. He went home and I went back to my condo to get things together. We went to see my family and to get back to making more money.

We went to Chicago for me to work their escort service. I called and got it hooked up. We took his girls, and they had a very good time. We drove two cars, my Mercedes-Benz, and his truck. We had a good time. We got there and checked into the rooms. We got two rooms. It was good.

My man took me on every call, and it was so much fun. We stayed for a week. We went shopping. We went on call after call. He said, "Baby, you are so fast. Stick and move". We are in Chicago. Move fast, get money, and we had to go back home to go to Las Vegas for the NBA to get more money. We flew there and checked into our hotel. But my life was changed.

Something Changed

I lost the desire to sell my body. So, I did not try to make any money. Something happened to me. It was because it was a challenge for me to make money in Las Vegas. That is my home, as well as Minnesota. That is where it all started. Big money. Millions of dollars.

When I look back on all the millions on top of the millions, getting into all the relationships I've been in, I ended up with nothing. I was getting to the point I was getting fed up. So, I made up my mind that I don't want to do this anymore.

I told him how I felt, and I said to him, "I'm done selling my body and if you don't like it, you sell your beef" and I meant that.

I called my husband, which was my top sugar daddy. We agreed that when he needs sex, he will get it and when I need money, I will get it or whatever I want or what he wants from me. That was before we got married. We had been married for at least 10 years and that time. So, he came from Iowa to talk to me. I had met my broker. Her name was Irene. She was the coldest that I know.

At that time, I had made up my mind that I was done with that lifestyle and so when my sugar daddy came up, as I prepared to tell him what I wanted to do, I asked God in secret what he wanted me to say. Then he spoke and said, "You will invest, and you will own property."

So, I told him that I would like to invest, and he said, "Okay". He said, "Okay, you go and find that house. Wherever you want it. It does not matter how much it cost. I will help you baby and I think it's a good thing and I will support you in anything you do because love you".

I said, "I gave God my life 100% and he wants me to be a good daughter and obey him." So, I want to do what you want me to do. So, now God was talking and showing me a lot. I started to listen, and I said, "Okay".

We went to dinner, and he wanted to do whatever made me happy. So, he went home, and I called him and told him what my main sugar daddy said. I wanted

Chapter 16
I'm Done with This

a big house, 15 to 20 rooms, six baths, full size, big everything. We looked and looked and did not like the ones I saw.

So, finally, he took me to a house in Farmington that was okay. It was one floor, two floors, and three floors on the top. It had a cold master room, a big bedroom, a jacuzzi, a full bath and showers, glass, and gold knobs.

The main floor had two bedrooms, a big living room, a beautiful sun porch, and a big patio. Under the porch was a big hot tub with seating for at least fifteen people and a two-car garage.

In the driveway, you can sit eight cars on the slab. It had a big kitchen and the house was fenced all around. The bottom floor was where we entertained our company. There was a bedroom, storage room, and a big theater room. Big sliding door that was made of glass.

I decided to buy the house. We did a big crystal chandelier in the foyer and my cars were a CLK430 Mercedes-Benz, a gold Jaguar, and a white Hummer. My man, I bought him, a white gold inside Jaguar and an XL Denali truck.

I had a 2009 Chrysler, black on black. I had a white Chrysler, and I had a red motorcycle. He had a big lime one. We had a big John Deere tractor, a pull one, and a big grill where you could put steak, fish, or whatever you wanted. We had all types of toolboxes.

My husband gave me power of attorney over everything he owned. I bought 3.11 million dollars worth of property. We went downtown to be registered with the state and he started to rent them out. We made at least $680,000 off the house. He bought three duplexes before he gave me power of attorney.

So, at that time, God had put me in a garment, and I was trying to be so good and walk this walk. I have never walked right or straight before or on the right path for God. I said to God that he has the wrong person and he said, "I have the right one and it is you".

I did not understand what God had spoken to me and so I began to pray. I started listening to the word of God and I prayed that God would take my bad language from me and stop my sleeping with men who are not my husband.

Chapter 16
I'm Done with This

I asked God to teach me what you are saying. Please make it plain to me. I was really confused. I'd already been to a Women's Conference in Orlando Florida. Women on the front line in my life were never the same.

During the preaching and teaching of the word of God, God spoke straight to my heart. He said to me, "I know she is one of the real women. She is a woman after God's own heart."

I trusted in God and things started going to the forefront of my head. Things started to come alive. God was moving in the spirit, and it was very deep, and I mean deep and scary.

But I trusted God with all my heart. I started speaking in places. I started speaking the word of God and God sent me to Waycross Georgia. I met my friend at the women's conference.

I stayed at Rosemont Hotel not that far from there. It was a 5-day conference. After the conference, God spoke to me again and said, "Go to Waycross". I told my friend. She said, "You better follow us" and we did.

So, God sent a prophetess with me, and it was hell getting there. Storm, rain, and hail, and the Hummer was rocking. It did everything but turnover. But we were okay.

I went there and it was a blessing. At that time, Charles was not feeling me at all. That was okay. I knew it was over because I chose God over him. At that time, he didn't do anything to me. God had told the prophet that I was chosen by God and anointed by him. To me, it was very serious. I'm not willing to go to hell for no human being.

Back Home

Back home, God spoke to me again and said, "To cut him off because Satan has sent him to suck the life out of you". For that very reason, I had to get rid of him, but my flesh said, "Huh". It was very hard for me, but I did it.

I sat there with Mona, she was the lady that God said to take care of her. I did. She lived with me for 2 years. She found God and learned how to put her whole armor of God on. She learned about the Holy Spirit.

Chapter 16
I'm Done with This

She was reading the Bible, learning to pray, learning about apostles, prophets, bishops and evangelists, and preachers. She learned what speaking into people's life meant, and she joined my church. It was good.

I was having closing after closing and was really trying to do the right thing. I did my last closing with Charles, but he never gave them the closing money. He was always lying in our relationship. He was a liar and a cheat. But it did not hit the fan until I had to go to prison. My whole life crashed in on me.

I put everything in storage. I put his name on it and when I got out, he had lost everything. I felt in my heart, that he took my stuff and put it in his daughter's house or sold it or put it in some lady's house. Everything I had was gone. I work so hard for what I had but when God speaks, listen.

CHAPTER 17
Dating Men with Power

I WORKED TO get knowledge about legal and non-legal sex houses. I traveled all over the world. I flew first class. I ate shrimp and drinks, and champagne, dressed as a businesswoman, and was drop-dead gorgeous and a glamor girl. When I walked, men stop and turned their heads. It was almost like they stopped breathing.

Some would give me a business card and I would do the same. All I have to do is show up. When I walk into the room, I was very quiet. I love to be seen but not heard because, for sure, I was a woman first and foremost.

I loved riding in Rolls-Royces, Mercedes-Benz, Maybach, Jaguars, Lamborghinis, Maserati, stingrays, Bentleys, limousine service, Excalibur, Lexus, and BW. I have drunk from the finest glasses and eaten from crystal gold plates, 24-carat gold, silverware, silk lace linen, piano, music, jazz playing, people sitting and making business deals, and investors making money. Wall Street.

We're talking stock, men wearing suits and bow ties and flying all over to meet tricks that are doing business with oil companies, banks, that own lawyers, judges, people working with the FBI, the police, and even doctors. Those were the kind of dates I was going on. I was dating all kinds of people.

Accountants and even owners of stores. I was always the one that did not deal with the help, always the owner. I have dates from China, Japan, Mexico, Italy, Asia, Korea, Vietnam, Jamaica, Indian, India, Iran, Portuguese, Laos, Whites, and Native Americans, and I have dated Jews, but no rabbis.

Chapter 17
Dating Men with Power

So, I have been with people from all walks of life. I have dated rich men, millionaire clothes designers, producers, models, writers, news broadcasters, realtors, brokers, and owners of million-dollar properties. I have dated mobsters and gangsters.

Take it to the House

So, let's go to the sex house. I dressed so well until I looked like a million dollars. I spent lots of money on my furs, lace, silk, features, diamonds, pearls, and rubies. I especially try to get into men's minds and get in their heads because if I have their minds, everything else will follow.

I especially like domination strap-ons and all different kinds of toys. I can work in a Dutch clap, nip clip, handcuffs, head mask, whips, and tools for the inside and cross-dressing.

If I had long sessions, they would start at $1,000. There were twelve women to choose from. Black, white, Korean, Asia, blonde, and they were all very beautiful, young, and sexy, and we were a family. When the doorbell rang, they would call the line.

I would keep eye contact with the potential clients at all times until I took my post and said my name,

"Mercedes". I would smile, my beautiful dark chocolate skin, my big brown eyes, and my pretty smile, pretty white teeth, with gold in my mouth that shined. I was five feet tall and weighed 132 pounds, with a very small 27-inch waistline. A very sexy woman with nice hair.

If they chose me, I smiled, took them by the hand, and walked them to my palace. It was a pretty condo. I spent a lot of money on my room to make it look like that. They would walk in, and their eyes would look like, "wow!"

I was so professional with everything I did and said. I would take their coat and jacket, or briefcase, and hang it up. Take my sheet from the door and cover my bed. Start on my strip and they wouldn't get naked. I would take their clothes off and then to the shower.

I would lay them down and put the big bright lights and check them with my gloves on to make sure they did not have any diseases. The girls and I went to the doctor every week and we were all good. So, for my safety, I needed to make sure that he was okay. I had to turn down thousands because of that. I needed to know them.

I would take my gloves and my clothes off, but I kept my lace stockings on. They could have been black, red, white, or gold. Once I got naked and start from their ears, down to his lips, and down to his bottom and down licking him all over until he began to say my name, making all kinds of noises, getting very emotional, starting to sweat, and shake. Then I would just caress his body until his mind was mine.

Then if his request was for 69 then, so be it, or cross-dress, or whatever it was. Then I would sit on him and watch him talk to me. Nice and slow, up, and down, then I start to move kind of fast, then I slow down but away to make sure he can see my face as he runs his hands all over me and my 38dd.

Then I would call my girl in. By the time she walked in, we are already up to $10,000. Now, I got him just where I want him. Now, I'm in control. Now, I put down what I do best.

I run my tongue up and down on him, with a condom on always. A very thin one when I'm giving him oral sex. But when I'm having sex, then blue for lubrication or a different one. It all depends on what I'm doing.

We had a bell that rang every hour because I need to know that he has money. When the bell rang, a knock on the door, drink coming, steak, crab, lobster, or whatever his heart desires.

A blonde girl would come into the room, and she knew automatically what to do and to say. She would take his credit card to the front. I would do that because he was my client. He would pay $2,000 to start. She loved to drink Jack Daniels and Coke and do some Krane. I would not because I was in recovery.

Yes, and I did not drink. I just made my daddy money. I was working it, baby! I was a hot mess, but I was a chocolate chip that you could eat, and it was delicious. I think the only thing I like was someone giving me oral sex.

We would get in the shower together. We would eat, drink, and have sex. My date gave me and her $5,000. Then I need my real man, who was not there, to have sex with me and dominate my mind.

I was not playing with my dates. We went swimming and just had good times. So, my blondie would take care of getting her cash. She was a bad girl. That was the way it was. We were two ice pieces together and we always made money. Every time I got picked or she got picked, it was a tag team.

That was my life in the bordello, it was oral sex with women and making money and pimps and prostitutes. So, I had lots of women. I took care of them. Life was good. I had five women at one time. So, I became a pimp. I had lots of different sides to me.

CHAPTER 18
Becoming a Minister in Prison

WELL, IT WAS on a Sunday that I spent a night with a girlfriend, Jasmine. When I woke up something had happened to me. I could not understand it at all. Because when I woke up, I said I have to find him. Now, remind you, I am going to be an ordained minister. I was wearing my garment, Christ robe. But I woke up thinking about a pimp. What the hell is going on? That's what I was thinking.

My friend said, "Are you sure you want to do this?" I'm a person others would never understand. But I don't always understand what's going on in my life.

Since 2005, when I said, "Yes" to God, so many things have come upon me. But God.

Back Down Memory Lane

So let me take you back to when I was in prison in 2008. I got out of prison on June 8, 2008, and went to work at Wendy on Lake Minnetonka. I worked for my sister in her cleaning business. We cleaned banks, everything.

I got to go to work release on April 20, then went to Mystic Casino on April 23, 2008. This day was different for me. I don't know what was going on, but I walked in, walk all around the casino, and chose a blackjack table. I sat first base, and no one was talking.

This man said, "Your name is Mercedes. I lost $130." I got up and as I got ready to leave, he said, "Do you want to gamble". I said, "Okay". He went to the machine to get more money and he kept asking me how much.

I said, "I'm not that person anymore and you don't know what you're asking me." He went on and on and we went to eat. We stayed there for about two hours and God allowed me to speak into his life.

He knew that I was a woman of God but kept trying to get me in bed. So, he went to the cash machine and got $500, and we had sex. I was not very happy about what I did. I felt like I had killed someone, and I threw up. I had sinned against God and my body was going through changes. As life went on, he said to me, "What's your store? Do you think that $10,000 would help?"

I said, "I don't know". He said, "Let me pray about it." So, he called me in two days and said, "Want me to help you?" So, he did. In three weeks, we had spent $30,000. We decided to write an agreement, that if my business is not profitable, I have five years to pay the money back.

Florida, Here I Come

Back to Mr. Florida. I drove to Florida by myself. I stopped in Arkansas to Marcus Mom's house. My ex was supposed to pay $315. I knew this was not going to work. So, my sister ended up paying it. It was not my ex's mom's business what was going on in my life. Her son and I did not make it for a good reason and that is from both sides, me, and him. It was no one's fault. It was our bad choices.

I love his mom to death, but she cannot control me like she does everyone else. So, I left and headed to Florida. Before I got there, I said to him, "Will you please get me a house or something of my own".

I met his mom. She lived in Rochester Minnesota. I also met his girls whom I love so much and still do. I have a bond with his mom.

One of his girls I knew from Nevada. We worked across the street in different houses. I made more than any woman in any house. I mastered this game. Thirty-four years of success. That's how he knew about me from the beginning. When I got to south Florida, he talked to me.

He took me into the house. We sat down and talked. I was very disappointed because right then and there he did not have me a place of my own. So, that didn't happen. He did have a problem getting me a wig. I went to the shop and spent at least $200 for hair, weave, getting my nails and my feet done, and a full body massage. It cost $110 for my nails and feet.

If I was going to wear a front lace wig, it would have been a human hair wig. But what was happening, he wanted to get $100,000 but he did not want to spend money to make money. It takes money to make money. You have to bring money to the table. So, everything was cheap.

A man or a pimp cannot tell you how to sell your body. You don't have what a woman has, and you never had a man get in bed with you because you are not a woman. That's why two women can make love to another woman because she is a woman and knows how to make her feel. So that is what it was. So, I was not happy about a prostitute who does not have one-third of my knowledge having control.

The devil is a liar. I wanted to find out if he was not what I thought. I knew it but I had to get the desire to go away and never come back. If I'm going to be back in the lifestyle again, I knew that I was going to be in and out. If I shut the store down, what could I do for him? He kept thinking I wanted to play. At that time, I had not played check or sold my body for four and a half years.

So, I would trick-check because I had a way of doing things without getting into trouble anymore. Then he was arguing with one of his girls. It was a lot of negativity and mess going on. Mess that I was no longer involved with. I still say that she was treating me, okay, but I'm not going to let anyone misuse me. Her son was my sweetheart and still is.

So, I left and went to my daughter's house. I have family all over the world. I have traveled to thirty-eight states. So, I know what I know. He tried to make me look like I was nothing. But what he didn't know is he never had a woman like me.

If you don't know how to use your body what does it mean? It means nothing. It's just like you can take a horse to water but you can't make him drink. But I can take a man's mind, make him drink, and then carry me anywhere I want to go.

So, I left and went to my daughter's house for three days. He called and asked me to come back. I thought things would be different, but it got worse. He started treating me very badly. Not going on calls. He wanted me to take the girls on calls. I knew I was out of there when the time was right.

The Pro Bowl was in January, so I left and prayed to God for forgiveness. I repented, fasted, and prayed. I got myself back to the right place and was done. God is good all the time. He helped me escape. I thank him.

I could go on and on but that's enough. I love him. If he needed prayer, I would pray for him. But that was it. If his mom needed me, I will always be there. For his kids as well. They are kids, yea.

My Time in the Scott County Jail

One day, I wrote a check for $53 in Missouri. I filled up my tank. I was driving my Hummer. I also got something to eat. That was in 2007. Then as time went on in 2010, I was in Shakopee, on my way to try to get over to the Hampton Inn, I went the wrong way.

As I was sitting at the red light the wrong way, I saw a police car. It was 1:05 a.m. I was just waiting until 2:00 a.m. to get $2,800 from the casino. I had to go there to get that kind of money, so I can go back home to Florida.

Before then, in Austin, I got arrested and taken to the Scott County Jail. That was on May 17, 2010, and I was there until May 31, 2010. Fourteen days later, here comes Missouri to get me on Memorial Day.

I was just thinking that if my daughter was still living. She would have been 28 years old. I was wondering how she would look and what she would be like. I wondered if she would have looked like me or her dad. So off to Jail I go.

I was so worn out by the time I made it to my cell. I rested as much as I could. I slept and I got up to eat breakfast. I met everyone. All the women were very nice to me. The CO was very nice.

Not the officer that arrested me, he was very mean to me. He was trying to get me on a prostitute case because my Vietnam friend, because I could not pronounce his name. He has fifty letters in his name.

When he was arresting me, I didn't know what he said and didn't care what he said. It was not true, so it didn't make it in court. I serve nineteen days there and Missouri came to get me. So, off I go to Missouri on May 31, 2010.

My Time in the Missouri jail

Well, I made it to Missouri, and oh my goodness, when I got there, I had never in my life seen a jail that looked like that. Oh, man! That's all I can say. I wanted to take off my feet. What I saw, I knew in my heart, it was going to be a long bit for me.

Chapter 18
Becoming a Minister in Prison

When I got inside, I thought I was in Africa, but I have never been to Africa before. Then I met Mrs. Boss because she was. She said to me, "Do you have weave in your head"? I said, "Yes". She said, "It has to come out". I said, "Put me in the hole because this hair cost $81 a pack, and I spent a lot of money on it".

She looked at me and said, "It is the way". She said, "Honey, I will help you. So, don't worry sweetie". She smiled at me and got her scissors to cut my hair.

She told the CO, who was in her office, to leave because she had to get this hair out of my head. It took us about three hours.

They had me in a cell with this white woman. I ended up praying for her. God used me. Then they gave me lice treatment. When I got to the door and walked in, oh my goodness. From the time I got in there, they put treatment on my hair.

Then one of the ladies gave me some shampoo. I was the only black person there and I felt kind of out of place. I have been around white people all my life. I was married to a white man for 11 years. So, being a woman of God, I have to take some things and have to swallow some things.

I'm going to be hit but I have to get up, dust myself off, and keep on moving. As time went on, we all came to be sisters in Christ, and kind of close. We leaned on each other after being there for 35 days.

So, getting to know the women, I began to pay attention to the women to see what was going on. I began to pray for them, myself, my ministries, my daughters, my grandkids, my sister, my brothers, and my leaders and his wife, family, and congregation.

Before I got there, they said nothing was happening. People were not going to court. Oh my, the Holy Spirit was moving. I began to see things.

I met this one lady, a woman of God. The next day, I went to court, and she left and went to another county. God started to move in that place through me like never before. It was awesome. I knew it was God.

We would sit down and talk. We would kid around. It had to be clean for me because I could not do anything that was against God. I had been delivered and God had taken so many things away from me. I have been clean for fifteen years. He took away prostitution for 32 years.

Chapter 18
Becoming a Minister in Prison

My bishop prophesied over my life. He told me what the Spirit said, and my life changed quickly. The move of the Spirit was upon me.

God took me and made me a different person. He began to deal with me. He took the desire for things that are not like him, away from me. He stripped me from everything that was hard to give up. I knew that I wanted to live for God.

I had a great desire in my heart. I wanted to know what the life of Christ was about. How does it feel to live only for God? But I know to go behind the veil, flesh cannot go there. No flesh can go to the Holy of Holies.

I wanted this very much. God changed my life in 2005, but I was not complete. I still had some desires that were not supposed to be in me. They were very personal things. Things that only me and God knew. So, I took it to him.

See, there are some things that, without a doubt, I need to take only to God. No sister or friend, but to God because people will judge you in a heartbeat. They will tell you how you are not right, but their marriage is a wreck.

They are not walking with God, and they are not where they need to be in God. But they want to tell you, that you don't need to be with a man or don't care how you feel about people. However, if you are doing what they want you to do, it's good. It is the reason I divorced my family and moved to Florida.

It did not look like God, but it was God. I knew some things were different about me. When I got up that morning, something took over me. My mind was very different. I love my family to death, but my family doesn't love for real. It is all fake. Just when they want something.

I don't care if my family doesn't talk to me when this book is out. This is my story. This is what I lived, went through, and been so hurt.

If I'm wrong, please, by all means, tell me how you love me, or else I don't want to hear it because your actions over the years have shown me. So, there you have it.

I love all of you, no matter what you have done to me or said about me. They talked about Jesus Christ. So, what? I'm no one. Amen.

These sisters of mine in jail, are very different. For my family, every time something happened to Maudell, everyone in the world knew about it. But I'm okay with it. Let me tell my business so that they won't tell the bishop things about me, and if there is anything he wants to know about anyone in his church, go to God or your members.

I want a bishop that has the time to know what is going on with his congregation and feels I have something that looked different. It doesn't matter if it is in the spirit realm or natural. I love the first lady. I feel like I just cannot connect with these people. I feel it's Satan.

But I will not give up because I trust them. I honor God first and foremost. Then I honor my bishop. I honor no man on this earth more than I honor my bishop and first lady. I trust them 100% with my life. I love them with all my heart and soul. I can't wait to be able to do what a daughter does for her spiritual father. So, to God be the glory.

CHAPTER 19
The Ladies Behind Bars

BELLA, WHEN I met her, she was a trip. She was not fair to Detra or anyone there. She took advantage of her. Detra had a sugar daddy, and she was the first person that said some positive things in my life. She was so nice to Bella. She bought her everything she asked for and even when she did not ask for something, she gave it to her. Detra has a heart of gold.

But Bella would go from one person to another talking about other people and it was not good. It got a lot of stuff started between people. Then she would act like nothing ever happened. As time went on, I prayed about every situation. I began to pray for Bella.

Detra had enough of her and did not want anything to do with her. She saw what was really going on with her. She saw the light and Detra started reading the Bible. Detra was a stripper in Missouri, so she had things going for her. She was a little Mercedes.

I loved her very much and I was not going to let anyone do her wrong. She is young enough to be my daughter and I had grown to love her. She is very sweet. Bella, on the other hand, was evil thinking, hateful, and acting like someone had done her wrong. But that was not the case. We cared for Bella and loved her as well, but she was too blind to see it.

So, time went on and I kept praying for Bella. I prayed that God would change her ways and make her into the person he wanted her to be and not who people wanted her to be. She was hurting, bitter, sad, mad, emotionally sick, and tired. She just had a whole lot of things in her that I knew she needed to be delivered from. I could recognize it because there are some of those spirits in me too, so that's how I knew.

Chapter 19
The Ladies Behind Bars

But things continue to happen. I talked to Detra because she was in her word and getting stronger each day. So, I would plant a seed in her with the word of God. She had great respect for me, and I knew she would listen because she truly wanted God to change her life. She did understand. She can read. She had completed college, so she can read. She had to get a great understanding of the Bible. Thank God for that. So, back to Bella.

I kept on praying and praying for Bella. I really loved on her too. She felt like no one cared for her. She needed attention as well. Detra got the attention and support she needed. So, I started spending time with her. No one understood why but it wasn't for them to know. I knew that God was going to move but I just didn't know how or when.

I kept the faith only in God, not in people. People will always 100% fail you but God never will. I talked to Detra about the right thing to do about the two situations and God worked it out. Then, it was good with them.

I know that God lives in the actions of the Holy Spirit. Action because the Holy Spirit is the teacher and trainer. It gets God's job done. Amen.

Miss Meadow was the one that bought me some shampoo when I first walked in. She was the nice one but not to anyone else. I had to talk and pray with her. The devil was trying to destroy her, and she knew it was Satan.

She had lots of things going on in her head and through prayer, God got her through. Her time came and she went home with her kids. She went to church and wrote Detra a ladder. That was very good, amen.

Now for FBI. They call her FBI because she used to work for them. So, you know no one talked to her about things. But we loved Miss FBI.

She was a very quiet, sweet lady, and she did not have money. So, Missy Larson gave her some noodles, so that bought attention to her, and the people started to give, and so did I.

She was a little lady. She liked to dance for the women. They gave her coffee or whatever she needed, so that was fun. I enjoyed it. It was very clean. She was still waiting for court.

Chapter 19
The Ladies Behind Bars

Brenda was a hot, hot, hot mess and had a mouth that would not wait for anything. She was hot as cayenne pepper, hot sauce, and every spice. She was hot as a firecracker, but she was a very sweet person.

At that time, she was 44 years old and had some hard knocks in her life. She was married to Satan as she said. But she was going through changes as she was doing her time. She was set to go home on August 3, 2010.

I miss her and continue to pray and keep in touch with her. God bless her, her boys and her husband, and everything she does. Keep her covered in your blood, amen.

For Rosalind, I really don't have a lot to say about her. She was a very standoff person. She tried to get into her word, and Satan was trying to attack me as I was fasting. But I said what I needed to say and left her alone.

So, I know it was from the enemy not from her. I forgave her and said if I offended her, I'm sorry. God bless her. Keep her covered, as well, in the name of Jesus, amen. To God be the glory. I love her as my sister.

Lucille was 22 years old, at that time, she was an ex-dancer. She got caught in some mess and had a 2-year bit. She already had 7 months in and so she a little trip. Sometimes I don't know what to think or say to her. She was a baby. She got herself in a little mess. But God is going to bless her. She was trying to be different. In some ways, I could see it. She had to grow. I prayed that she would get her bond with her parents.

I prayed that everything worked out with her and her boyfriend. I prayed that one day he would become her husband. He bought her a beautiful ring, and they were supposed to get married.

So, I pray that his family came around and understands that this is his life. If he makes a mistake just be there for him and support their son. Don't put him in a place where he must choose between his wife and parents. It should be his wife because that's the way that God sees it.

Good luck Lucille. I love you, little sister. May God bless you and everything you do.

Aaliyah, she was bunkers, and she was a trip. She was a check writer, for real. Aaliyah had to go to six different countries, from jail to jail. She beat every case and was on her way to the last one. She was an okay person. I don't have much to say but God had work to do in her if she let him. I pray that everything is well with her. May God bless her and keep her covered under the blood.

Mackenzie was a woman in jail with me. She was a very beautiful woman. She reminds me of my first love, the woman that turned me out, that's who she reminded me of even as I'm walking with the Lord. I fell in love with her for a long time. I still remember, honestly.

But I am sold out for God. I'm on a mission for God but she was so sweet to me and in the few words she said, "You are the last person I want to be in an argument with." So, I knew she had great respect for me.

Ever since then, I have had great love for her. Thank God I'm saved because it changed a whole lot of trouble for me. She was the type to hit. I respect her as my sister in Christ Jesus.

Mackenzie, I prayed that I would see her at the Women's Conference in August 2011. I prayed that anyone who wanted to reach me and come to the conference would have called Ticketmaster in downtown Minnesota.

God bless you, and keep you, your husband, and your kids covered in the blood of Jesus. I will never forget you. Know the Lord and savior. Make up in your mind, that you're going to live for God. If you line up, your family will line up for God.

Miss Kristin was right about everything. Besides she was my sister. I cared a lot about her. I prayed that God allowed her to show herself approved to her family and kids. She and that Gucci man. He was her towel boy.

At that time, she was waiting for her husband, so you know how that goes. I pray that God has given her a man that loves her and has given her everything she wants in life. May God keep her and break her. I pray that she is in a place where someone needs to hear her pray.

Brenda, my sweet sister in Christ Jesus. I love you Brenda, more than you ever know. You have a very good heart. You just got yourself caught up in some mess but that was the most beautiful letter I have ever had.

Chapter 19
The Ladies Behind Bars

Thank you, my sweetheart and I hope you served your time and got home to your kids and hugs. If you had to go to another county always remember this, God will go everywhere you go. He said he will never leave you nor forsake you, in Jesus name.

I love you Brenda forever and ever. I pray that God keeps you and covers you in the blood of Jesus our Lord. Amen.

Miss St. Clair, my sister. When I first laid eyes on you, I knew you were a very sweet person. I'm so glad that I met you. I'm sorry to be this way, but only God. I want to say first and foremost, God bless your kids, your mom, and your family.

I hope I live to see the day you say, "Yes" to God. I pray by the time this book comes out you will be home with your family. This cannot happen to you again. You have to take a very good look at yourself and know what God needs to take away from you. You have to know what is wrong in you and be ready for God to move.

Get caught up in the rapture my sister. I say this because I love you like a sister or as if you are my daughter. I am old enough to say that and be your mom. Think about your kids and what you want for them and what you want out of life.

I hope and pray one of the things you want is God and that you want your kids to be children of God. May God bless you and keep you, and keep you covered in the blood of Jesus. Amen.

Sue Carla thought she was a Barbie. For real. She was a pornstar, real story. She was here with us, and she was okay. She thought more of herself than anyone else.

She was a very sweet person to me. I cared a lot about her. No matter where I was, she would sit next to me if no one else was sitting there. Women would always sit and listen to the word of God because that's all they talked about. I always glorified God.

She was drawn to me through God. The true and living God that dwells in me. She got out. But I have all the women's phone numbers or email addresses. So, it was a good thing that God let me come here. It was a blessing.

If I could, I would do it all over again. God bless you, Sue, and be with you in the name of Jesus.

Hello Viola. God bless you. First and foremost, I feel you are a very good person with a very good heart. I liked you when I first saw you. I just wanted something to say. So, God made a way for me to be in your life and I'm glad I'm in your life.

I'm so glad God put you and your sister back together. I prayed and prayed unto God to move. God answers prayer. So, keep praying. keep God first and stay in your word and stay clean.

Nichole, God bless you, your little sister, and your big sister. I'm so glad God put you all back together. Your mom is a very sweet person. I pray that everything worked out with your family. I pray that you let God change you in every way and wash your mouth and change your way of thinking. I pray that God takes everything that is not like him out of you.

Never let anyone turn you against your sister because blood is thicker than water. Your sister loves you. If you have a disagreement with your sister or family, go and make it right. Prayer does work. Ask God to please fix it in the name of Jesus. Love always.

Miss Layla, when you came in, you were a mess. You thought everyone was against you. You wanted to fight Bella. You did not care for her at all. You and Bella got into it so many times, but Layla, you did not back down at all.

Bella was not tough as she claimed to be, so it all came out who was really tough. But Layla, you liked me and wanted me to pray for you. You had great respect for me, and I had respect for you. I hope everything is well with you, your kids, and your family. I pray that God take drugs out of your life and bless your husband and make him the man he made him to be.

For my Vanessa, I hope and pray that you are doing well my sister. I love you and miss you so much. You are holy (smile). God is good all the time. No matter what you got to go through in life, remember God is with you always. He will never leave you, nor forsake you. God is not a man that he should lie. There is no fault in him.

So, keep praying. Keep the faith. Keep your eyes on God, not man. If you fall down get back up again, dust yourself off, and follow God. Tell your mom, "God bless her, keep her, and make it right with your dad". No matter what he has done, forgive my daughter. Your chocolate chip. Love always. May God keep you, in the name of Jesus.

Well, Miss Hazel, you were a mess when I first laid eyes on you. You looked like you were demon-possessed but God gave me the strength and power to pray and deal with you. God is able to heal. God bless you and keep you. Be safe and no matter what you do, keep it holy.

Miss Dee, you are first of all, very sweet and funny and have jokes. They are funny. I really like you as my sister in Christ Jesus. I miss you and love you. May God bless you and keep you in Jesus mighty name

I'm so glad that I met each of you. I'm sorry to be the way that I was. I hope I live to see the day each of you says, "Yes" to God. I pray by the time this book comes out you are home with your families.

So, keep praying. Keep the faith. Keep your eyes on God, not man. If you fall down get back up again, dust yourself off, and follow God. I hope and pray one of the things you want is God and that you want your kids, family, friends, and loved ones to be children of God.

I miss each of you and continue to pray for you all. Some of you, I have been able to keep in touch with and for that I am grateful. May God bless you and keep you, and keep you covered in the blood of Jesus.

God changed my life and if he did it for me, he will definitely do it for you. Amen!

CLOSING PRAYER

I THANK MY Lord and Savior, Jesus Christ, and the Holy Spirit for giving me another chance in life. For keeping me and saving my life. I thank you for breath. I thank you for the breath of life. I thank you for your rivers of water that never run dry.

I praise you for being God all by yourself. You are the Holy One. You are a just God. You are Alpha and Omega. You are the beginning and the end. The first and the last. I praise you for being perfect. I love you God with all my heart, mind, and soul.

I thank you for showing me how to talk, to walk, and for your power manifesting in me. Finish what you started in me. Raise me up for the nations. I know I will be very knowledgeable in you because if you spoke it, and it hasn't come to pass, God your word will not come back to you void. There are no lies in you. You are so perfect.

To all of the men that were in my life and had a personal relationship with me, you know who you are.

This is for you to know that God is God. I thank God for letting me cross your path. What He has allowed me to go through, my bad choices, I thank him for his grace and mercy.

What you did to me, you have done it to God, if I have hurt any of you in any way, please forgive me. If you have not given your life to Christ, do so at this time. Repent, ask for forgiveness, and ask God to come into your life.

Believe that Jesus died and rose from the dead, and he lives. Allow him to come into your heart. If you have done this, then you are saved. If you need to be born again, then do so at this time. God bless you.

May God change your life
just as he changed mine.

Amen!

Made in the USA
Middletown, DE
28 January 2023

22742765R00157